Eden to Eternity

THE CHRONOLOGICAL STORY
OF SCRIPTURE

VOLUME 3

THE DAILY GRACE CO.

INTRODUCTION

One of the primary subjects we study in school is history. While many enjoy the study of history, others may view this subject as boring or unnecessary. But we learn history so we can remember. Time keeps moving forward, and the more time progresses, the easier it becomes to forget what happened in the past. History books are designed to help us remember the past, and these books are structured so we can learn about the past in a certain order. If events were not described in the order of their occurrence, we would have to work harder to put the pieces of history together. Learning about events in the order they happened also helps us understand how past events shape our present circumstances. If we jump to the present without considering the past, we are unable to have as great an appreciation and understanding of what led us to today.

A record of events written in the order of their occurrence is called a chronology. The Bible typically groups books of the Bible by genre, and while many of these books happen to be in chronological order, the Bible as a whole is not arranged in chronological order. While the Bible can be understood in the way it is arranged, studying the Bible chronologically is similar to studying a history book. When we study the Bible chronologically, we are able to better understand how the events of biblical history began and unfolded over time. In addition to that, the Bible is about God, and studying the Bible chronologically allows us to see God's plans progress, His character revealed, and His promises fulfilled. And most of all, studying the Bible chronologically helps us see that the Bible is a unified story that points us to Jesus.

Note:

The arrangement of this study material is based on approximate dating and scholarly insight. While the arrangement may differ from other chronological plans, the order was thoughtfully and intentionally placed together to be as faithful as possible to biblical history.

In addition to a differing chronological timeline, some resources from The Daily Grace Co., such as The Bible Handbook, *note when each book of the Bible was written and recorded, which could sometimes be decades or even hundreds of years after an event happened. However, this study is organized based on the approximate time each event actually occurred.*

Elisha to Malachi
— VOLUME 3 TIMELINE —

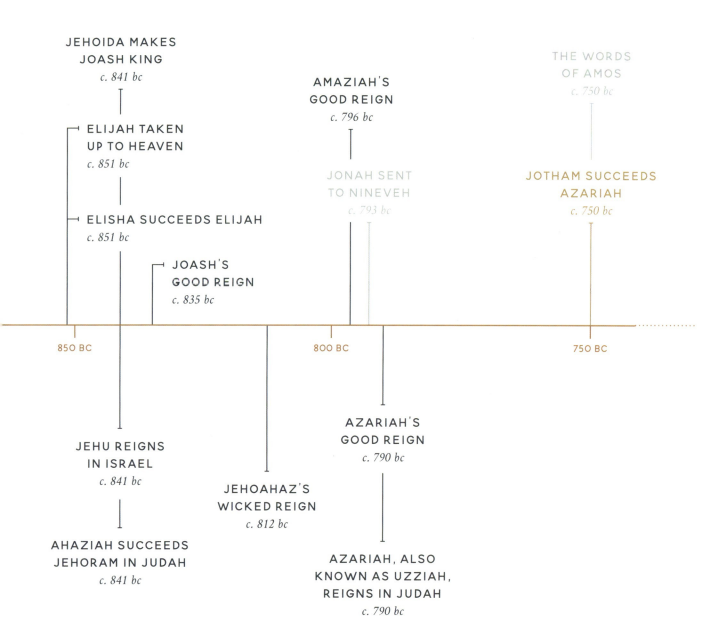

c. (circa) = approximately

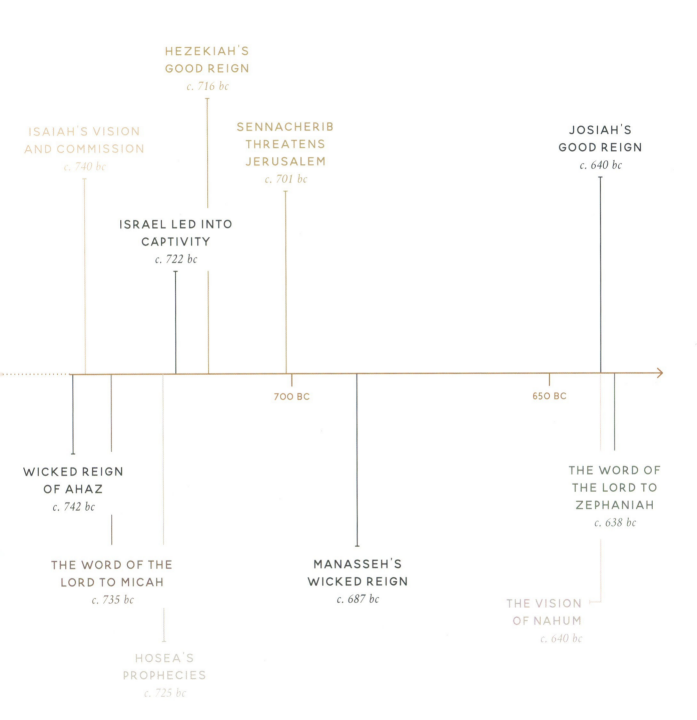

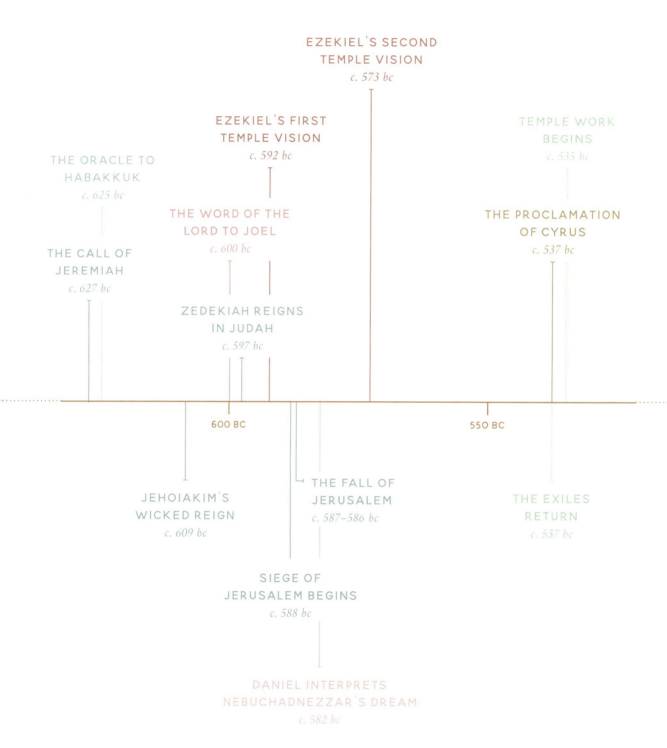

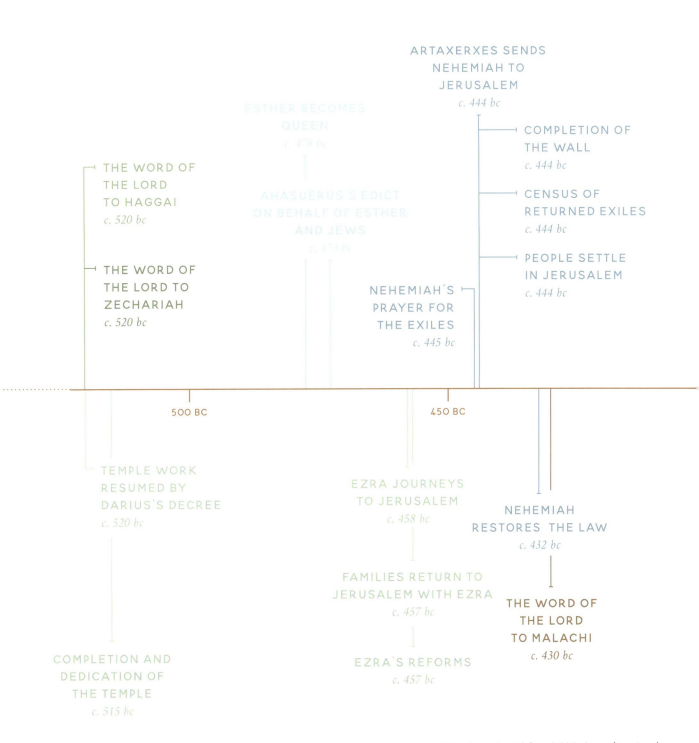

EDEN TO ETERNITY: VOLUME 3

While parts of history make us celebrate, there are also parts of history that can make us cringe. At this point of redemptive history, Israel's actions certainly cause us to shudder. God's plan for His people was to form them into a thriving, holy nation under His rule. But His people have abandoned God's ways and refused to give Him the worship He deserves. The sin of Israel's leaders has caused the kingdom of Israel to divide into two opposing kingdoms. Evil leaders rule, and God's people are wayward and wicked. The wickedness of Israel and Judah's leaders, as well as the wickedness of the people themselves, causes God to send prophets to encourage their repentance through warnings of judgment. Although God's people reject God and pursue idol worship, God is faithful and merciful to give them opportunities to repent and warnings of His judgment if they do not repent.

This chapter in redemptive history contains all the prophets God sent to Israel and other nations connected to Israel. Though these prophecies of impending judgment may be hard to read, these prophecies speak to the seriousness of sin and our just God. Though this section seems to be one major downward spiral for God's people, God will remain faithful to His covenant. Sprinkled between prophecies of judgment are promises of hope and restoration. God will not leave His people battered and broken—He will save and restore them through a coming Messiah, who will unite God's people and transform their hearts.

Contents

INTRODUCTION & TIMELINE   2–8

2 KINGS	10–13, 16–21, 26, 36, 42, 62–65, 84, 90, 118
OBADIAH	14
PSALMS	14, 42, 60–65, 68, 122, 188, 214
2 CHRONICLES	18–21, 26, 36, 42, 62, 84, 90, 118
JONAH	22
AMOS	28–31
ISAIAH	32–35, 44–51, 58–83
MICAH	38
HOSEA	52–55
NAHUM	86
ZEPHANIAH	92
JEREMIAH	94–119, 126–133
HABAKKUK	124
LAMENTATIONS	134–139
EZEKIEL	140–175
JOEL	176
DANIEL	178–187
EZRA	188–191, 206
HAGGAI	192
ZECHARIAH	194–199
ESTHER	202–205
NEHEMIAH	208–215
MALACHI	216

WHAT IS THE GOSPEL?   218

2 Kings 1–4

Editor's Note: Eden to Eternity: Volume 2 *ended with us learning about the history of Judah's kings in 2 Chronicles, along with the hope of the Davidic line being continued through the young King Joash. As we begin Volume 3, we will take a short break from the storyline of 2 Chronicles to catch up on what is happening in the northern kingdom of Israel and Israel as a whole during this time period, starting with the rule of Ahaziah and Elisha's succession of Elijah.*

SECOND KINGS OPENS SHORTLY AFTER THE DEATH OF THE EVIL KING AHAB OF ISRAEL.

His son Ahaziah begins to reign over Israel in his father's place. However, the text quickly informs us of his injury and subsequent inquisition to Baal-zebub. Instead of turning to the Lord in his distress, Ahaziah went to a false god, and Elijah quickly confronted him for seeking hope apart from the Lord. Elijah prophesies that Ahaziah will die, and that prophecy quickly comes true.

In chapter 2, a chariot of fire appears, and Elijah is taken to heaven in a whirlwind. Interestingly, there is no mention of death in Elijah's story. Elisha enters the scene as Elijah's replacement, watching as his predecessor is called up to heaven. This is displayed as Elisha asks, "Where is the Lord God of Elijah?" (2 Kings 2:14). After asking this question, Elisha strikes the water, and it parts before him. It is clear that God is with Elisha as he steps into his role as prophet.

Chapter 3 reintroduces us to Joram, the son of Ahab, who is now king over Israel, and also to Jehoshaphat, the king of Judah. Elisha proclaimed the Word of the Lord to these kings as they fought together against Moab, and the Lord showed mercy because Jehoshaphat followed the Lord.

Chapter 4 shows Elisha performing miracles, proclaiming the truth, and having compassion for those in need. From providing an abundance of oil for a poor widow to providing a son for a barren woman, God is a God who provides. This chapter shows us the love and compassion of God in raising the Shunammite woman's son from the dead. Despite the great sin and difficulty of this time in Israel's history, God is still at work, and He is calling out a faithful remnant of people to love and serve Him.

These passages point us to our need and desire for a better king. Jesus is that King. Even good kings like Jehoshaphat were riddled with flaws and sinful choices. Elijah prophesied God's judgment for sin, but Jesus is the true and better prophet who bore the judgment of God in our place. Elisha, through God's power, parted the waters before him, but Jesus, by His own power, would still the raging storms. Elisha spoke the Word of God, but Jesus is the Word made flesh (John 1:14). There is only one prophet who can redeem, and that is Jesus, who is our hope and Redeemer.

God is a God who provides.

THE PEOPLE OF ISRAEL AND JUDAH LIVED UNDER EVIL KINGS. YET GOD WAS STILL WORKING IN THE NATION DESPITE THE EVIL LEADERS. HOW DOES THIS ENCOURAGE YOU IN TIMES YOU EXPERIENCE UNFAIR OR UNJUST LEADERSHIP?

In biblical times, the oldest son would typically receive a double portion of the family inheritance. Elisha asks Elijah for a double portion of the Spirit that was on Elijah to be on him. Elisha was unconcerned with material wealth. He wanted to speak and minister with the power of God.
WHAT ARE YOUR PRIORITIES IN LIFE? WHAT DO YOU MOST WANT? PHYSICAL OR SPIRITUAL BLESSING?

The miracle of raising the Shunammite's son performed by Elisha shows a picture of how we are all dead in our sins, yet through God's power, we can be raised to new life. Just as Elisha stretched himself over the boy's entire body, salvation and new life in Christ affect every part of us.
WHAT ARE SOME WAYS THAT THE SALVATION OF GOD HAS IMPACTED YOUR LIFE?

2 Kings 1–4

2 Kings 5–8

GOD IS FAITHFUL. HE ALWAYS KEEPS HIS PROMISES.

In 2 Kings 5, we read the story of Naaman, a man who was healed of his leprosy through the urging of a young servant girl. In this account, we see the commander of Israel's enemy being healed and placing his faith in Yahweh. There is a stark contrast between Naaman's story and Gehazi's story. An Israelite servant of the prophet Elisha, Gehazi was afflicted with leprosy due to his greed and deceit. God calls His own from every nation, and even here in Israel's history, we can see the grafting in of those once far from Him. God does not always work how we expect, yet He always proves Himself to be faithful.

These chapters in 2 Kings remind us that God cares about the details. Chapter 6 opens with an example of God's compassion, even in something as simple as losing a borrowed item. Just like the prophet Isaiah, Elisha is often called "the man of God" (2 Kings 6:6, 9, 10, 15). Elisha prayed his servant would see the Lord's protection (2 Kings 6:17), then he prayed that their enemy would become blind (2 Kings 6:18). Then, upon the capture of their enemy, Elisha calls for a feast. What a beautiful picture of the gospel. We who were once God's enemies are now invited to feast at His table. The story of Elisha causes us to look to Jesus. He is the One who heals, loves, and shows compassion toward all those who come to Him in faith.

Chapter 6 concludes with the siege of Samaria, where there was a severe famine. But in 2 Kings 7, Elisha boldly proclaims that they would soon see God's deliverance. Though his words seemed unbelievable, every word of Elisha's prophecy came true. God was faithful to His servant Elisha and to His chosen people. This type of provisional care is highlighted in 2 Kings 8. The same Shunammite woman who was introduced in chapter 4 is back. During the time of famine, she and her family fled in obedience to Elisha's instructions. When they came back, the king heard how Elisha had provided for her. He restored everything that belonged to her family and more. God abundantly provides for His people; He is faithful.

> God does not always work how we expect, yet He always proves Himself to be faithful.

ELISHA IS CALLED "THE MAN OF GOD" THROUGHOUT THE TEXT.
WHAT CAN WE LEARN FROM ELISHA'S FAITH IN THESE CHAPTERS?

IN 2 KINGS 7, THE CAPTAIN DID NOT BELIEVE GOD WOULD DELIVER THEM.
WHEN DO YOU STRUGGLE TO BELIEVE IN GOD'S GOODNESS TOWARD YOU?

REFLECT ON 2 KINGS 8:19. HOW DOES THIS INFORM OUR UNDERSTANDING OF
GOD'S COVENANTAL FAITHFULNESS?

Obadiah
Psalms 82–83

Editor's Note: Today, we take a break from the storyline of 2 Kings to turn to Obadiah. Obadiah was a prophet of God who prophesied around 848 BC, just after Elisha succeeded Elijah and during the time when evil kings ruled Israel. Additionally, we are discussing Psalms 82–83. While we cannot date these psalms to this time period with absolute certainty, these psalms are relevant to what is happening in Obadiah and were likely written around the same time, which is why they are placed here.

OBADIAH IS THE SHORTEST OLD TESTAMENT BOOK, YET IT IS STILL FULL OF TRUTH ABOUT GOD'S JUDGMENT OF SIN AND THE DELIVERANCE OF HIS PEOPLE.

This book is unique as Obadiah is one of just a few prophets who did not prophesy against Israel or Judah. Instead, the book focuses on the nation of Edom, which was founded by Jacob's brother, Esau. The nation had been at odds with God's people for generations. Edom's most recent crime against God's people had occurred during the Babylonian invasion. When Jerusalem and the cities of Judah were invaded, Edom plundered the cities and even captured and killed some of Judah's refugees.

The book of Obadiah reminds us that God is sovereign in the affairs of men. Nations rise and fall at His command. The nation of Edom had grown strong. In their pride, they believed that nothing could hurt them (Obadiah 3). However, in His justice, God would judge their sin.

Obadiah presents Edom's pride and subsequent fall as a picture of the pride and fall of all nations and people. Edom is not the only prideful nation. Pride has affected all human beings since they were born. And, if we follow in the footsteps of Edom, indulging in our pride and placing ourselves in a higher position than we ought to, we will meet the same end. No nation or person is self-sufficient. We all depend on God's mercy to give us breath each day. Praise the Lord that He delivers us from our pride and gives us new hearts that can see and understand the truth of the gospel. The end of the book of Obadiah gives us a glorious promise that the Lord's kingdom will be established. We can take comfort in knowing that He will be faithful, and He will reign forever.

Asaph, who was a chief musician in David's court, uses both lament and prophecy in Psalm 82 as he mourns the wicked rulers of the earth and points readers to the future judgment of God. God appoints human rulers to lead with righteousness, but these rulers often do the opposite of what God intends. While human authorities may fail, God does not, and He will judge the earth in righteousness.

Psalm 83 is another of Asaph's psalms, and it contains both lament and a call for God to destroy Israel's enemies. Throughout Israel's history in the Old Testament, nation after nation tried to annihilate them, but God always delivered them. Because of Jesus, we also can trust God to deliver us from our enemies. We live in a world that is hostile toward the gospel, but the truth of Jesus will always prevail.

IN WHAT AREAS OF LIFE DO YOU FEEL SELF-SUFFICIENT? KNOWING THAT GOD PROVIDES EVERYTHING YOU HAVE, INCLUDING THE BREATH IN YOUR LUNGS, LIST EIGHT TO TEN WAYS YOU ARE DEPENDENT ON GOD TO GET THROUGH TODAY.

JAMES 4:6 SAYS, "GOD RESISTS THE PROUD BUT GIVES GRACE TO THE HUMBLE." WRITE A PRAYER ASKING GOD TO HUMBLE YOU.

CONSIDER THE HUMILITY OF JESUS. HE TOOK ON THE LIKENESS OF HUMANITY AND CHOSE TO SERVE MANKIND, EVEN TO THE POINT OF HIS DEATH (PHILIPPIANS 2:5–11). WHAT CAN YOU LEARN FROM JESUS'S HUMILITY? IN WHAT WAYS CAN YOU IMITATE JESUS'S HUMILITY IN YOUR LIFE?

2 Kings 9–10

Editor's Note: After reading Obadiah yesterday, today, we turn back to 2 Kings, where we continue to learn about the evil kings who ruled over the northern kingdom of Israel during this time period.

AS WE READ ISRAEL'S HISTORY AND, IN PARTICULAR, THE EVENTS SURROUNDING ITS KINGS, WE WILL CONTINUE TO COME ACROSS SOME DIFFICULT AND WEIGHTY PASSAGES.

Over and over again, we see evil kings reign over Israel and Judah. Kings and their families are murdered, and new kings are anointed to reign. The beginning of 2 Kings 9 shows us that a new king, Jehu, has been anointed to rule Israel.

As a part of his commissioning as king, Jehu is told to kill the family of King Ahab to avenge the murder of the prophets (1 Kings 18:4). It can be hard to fully understand the purpose behind such brutal acts of violence. But we know God is good as He deals with sin and idolatry seriously. He is a God jealous for the worship that belongs to Him alone. After the gruesome demise of Jezebel, Jehu sets his sights on Ahab's sons in chapter 10. We can see that Jehu was a cunning king who worked to rid the nation of Ahab's descendants, as well as the prophets of Baal. God commended Jehu's obedience in removing evil and idolatrous influences. Unfortunately, we also later see that Jehu did not tear down the shrines where priests made offerings to false gods and continued in the sins of Jeroboam. Second Kings 10:31 tells us that Jehu "was not careful to follow the instruction of the Lord God of Israel with all his heart." Sadly, this was true of so many of the kings.

Despite the wickedness of the kings who came after Jehu, God would be faithful to His covenant. God made a promise, and He would keep it. This is the promise of the One who would come from David's line. It is the promise of the Messiah. God would be faithful to His people by sending Jesus—the answer to the sin, suffering, and brokenness found in the pages of these historical books and the hearts of all humanity. Throughout these chapters, we see the magnificent faithfulness of God. Even when we stray, He is faithful. God's love for His people has never wavered. He is sure and steadfast. It is His great love that compels us to serve Him with our lives and rest in confident assurance that, as He has always been faithful, He will continue to be faithful to us.

> God's love for His people has never wavered. He is sure and steadfast.

HOW WOULD YOU SUMMARIZE JEHU'S REIGN?

THESE CHAPTERS REMIND US OF THE SERIOUSNESS OF IDOLATRY AND SIN. WHAT THINGS ARE YOU TEMPTED TO ELEVATE ABOVE GOD? IN OTHER WORDS, WHAT ARE THE THINGS YOU FEEL YOU CANNOT LIVE WITHOUT? SPEND SOME TIME JOURNALING AND CONFESSING THOSE THINGS TO THE LORD.

WHAT DOES IT LOOK LIKE TO UNDERSTAND DIFFICULT PASSAGES IN LIGHT OF WHAT IS TRUE ABOUT GOD?

2 Kings 11–13
2 Chronicles 24

Editor's Note: Now that we have caught up on Israel's kings and prophets during this time period, we return to the story of the evil Athaliah and the power struggle she sparked in Judah. If this sounds familiar, that is because we first caught a glimpse of this story in our study of 2 Chronicles 21–23 in Eden to Eternity: Volume 2. *As the narrative timelines for the northern and southern kingdoms converge once again, we return to this record to see how God worked through unlikely circumstances to preserve the Davidic covenant in Judah.*

AFTER JEHU'S REIGN, THINGS WENT DOWNHILL FAST.

In 2 Kings 11, the story returns to the kingdom of Judah, where we are introduced to a young woman named Jehosheba, who was also referred to as Jehoshabeath in 2 Chronicles 22:11. Though she is largely unknown, she plays a critical part in the story of Scripture. As you may remember from studying 2 Chronicles 21–23 in *Eden to Eternity: Volume 2*, the evil Athaliah, who was Ahaziah's mother, set out to kill all of the descendants of David and make herself ruler. But Jehosheba took Joash, her young nephew, and hid him in the temple for six years. He was hidden until the time was right for him to become king.

Joash was only seven years old when he became king (2 Chronicles 24:1). During his kingship, Joash did what was right in the eyes of the Lord under the instruction of the priest Jehoiada, with much of his reign focused on repairing the temple. However, Joash allowed false worship to continue in the high places (2 Kings 12:2–3). This may seem like an odd and insignificant story, but we must remember that this is the line through which Jesus was promised to come. God in His sovereignty would not allow the Davidic line to be destroyed. He would use a young woman determined to live courageously to preserve the line of the Messiah. God does not neglect His covenant. He is faithful to His word.

These chapters recount for us king after king in Israel and Judah. Some were certainly better than others, but each was riddled with problems. Second Kings 13 begins with Jehoahaz in Israel. Like many of the evil kings, we are told that he did what was evil in the sight of the Lord, yet Jehoahaz turns to the Lord on behalf of the people. And God is merciful. The text says that God gave Israel a deliverer. The sovereign Lord cared for and delivered His people.

Sadly, the people did not repent of their wickedness. But God is a covenant-keeping God. These historical narratives point us toward His steadfast love for His people, even when they are living in direct opposition to His Word. Through kings, prophets, and even ordinary people like Jehosheba, God continually pursued His people and provided a way for His people to come back to Him. In Christ, God provided a way for us to be made right before a holy God. Let us rejoice in God's faithfulness and loving pursuit of His people.

HOW DOES THE STORY OF JEHOSHEBA ENCOURAGE YOU TO STEP OUT IN FAITH?

WHAT ARE SOME EXAMPLES OF GOD USING ORDINARY PEOPLE FOR HIS PURPOSES, BOTH IN ISRAEL'S HISTORY AS WELL AS YOUR OWN STORY?

HOW IS GOD'S SOVEREIGNTY MADE EVIDENT IN THESE CHAPTERS?

2 Kings 14
2 Chronicles 25

THROUGHOUT ISRAEL'S HISTORY, MANY KINGS WOULD RISE AND FALL, AND KING AFTER KING WOULD DO EVIL.

Occasionally, one of the southern kings is described as being a good ruler. Second Kings 14 and 2 Chronicles 25 present the account of Amaziah, king of Judah. He was the son of Joash, and Scripture says that he did what was right in the eyes of the Lord. But like many of the kings who came before him and many who would succeed him, Scripture also points out that he did not do so wholeheartedly.

Amaziah's pride was on full display during his kingly reign. As soon as he was king, Amaziah killed the servants who had gone up against his father. Interestingly, Scripture records that he did not kill the children of the conspirators according to the Law. While preparing for battle, Amaziah paid to have the army of Israel join him, but a man of God stepped in and warned him not to have the Israelites' army join in the battle, for "the Lord is not with Israel" (2 Chronicles 25:7). Though Amaziah lost the money that he had paid and thousands of additional Israelite soldiers, he still achieved victory by God's mercy.

However, when God provided the king with victory over the Edomites, instead of worshiping God out of gratitude, Amaziah worshiped the false gods of those he defeated. He also allowed false worship to continue at the high places. When God sent a prophet to call the king of Judah back to holy living, Amaziah pridefully rejected the words of the prophet. As a result of his idolatry, the Israelite army defeated him.

With each new king we read about, we hope he will be the one to turn things around for God's people. Perhaps he will finally seek God's will and rule justly. However, we are often let down by each ruler. Our hearts long for justice and restoration. That longing is fulfilled in the only ruler who has never failed—Jesus Christ. Unlike the long line of human kings who continually failed, King Jesus's reign will never end.

> Our hearts long for justice and restoration. That longing is fulfilled in the only ruler who has never failed—Jesus Christ.

GOD INTERVENED TO PROVIDE VICTORY FOR KING AMAZIAH, AS SEEN IN 2 KINGS 14. HOW HAS GOD INTERVENED IN YOUR OWN LIFE?

AMAZIAH'S PRIDE PREVENTED HIM FROM HEARING GOD'S CALL TO REPENT AND TURN TOWARD HIM. SPEND SOME TIME IN REFLECTION, ASKING THE LORD TO ROOT OUT SINS LIKE PRIDE OR SELF-SUFFICIENCY THAT CAN KEEP YOU FROM EXPERIENCING CLOSE FELLOWSHIP WITH HIM.

HOW DID KING JESUS SUCCEED WHERE THE OTHER KINGS FAILED?

2 Kings 14, 2 Chronicles 25

Jonah 1–4

Editor's Note: Today, we take a break from the narrative of 2 Kings and 2 Chronicles to study the story of Jonah, a prophet who lived during this time period in redemptive history.

THE BOOK OF JONAH IS A SHORT STORY ABOUT A REBELLIOUS PROPHET WHO TRIES TO RUN FROM GOD.

In the first verses of the book, the Lord tells Jonah to go to Nineveh, the capital of Assyria. Assyria was one of Israel's greatest enemies, and the Lord eventually uses Assyria to exile Israel for judgment for their sin. When Jonah hears God's call, he boards a ship that is heading to Tarshish, the opposite direction of Nineveh. However, once on the ship, God sends a great storm to hinder Jonah's voyage. Jonah is soundly sleeping as he is awakened by frantic sailors fearing for their lives and wondering how they will survive.

As they cast lots to see who is responsible for bringing about this mighty storm, the lot falls on Jonah. The sailors were terrified, for they knew that Jonah was running from God. They ask him what to do, and Jonah tells them to hurl him into the sea because he is the reason behind the storm. In His mercy, God allows Jonah to be swallowed by a great fish. He spends three days and three nights in its belly, praising God for delivering him from the sea. After being spit out, Jonah goes to Nineveh as God told him to do. God has given Jonah another chance.

When Jonah tells the people of Nineveh about the coming judgment of God, the people repent immediately. Rather than rejoice in their salvation, Jonah grew bitter and angry. He tells the Lord that this was why he ran in the first place. Jonah knew God was compassionate and loving and that He would extend His forgiveness to the evil people in Nineveh (Jonah 4:2).

The Lord questions Jonah's anger and asks why He should not care for a city of many people. As God questions Jonah, we must also ask this question of ourselves. Do we desire that all people, friend or foe, be saved and know the truth of the gospel? Like Jonah, we can become bitter when we see God's goodness in the lives of those whom we deem do not deserve it. But that is our story—while we were still sinners, Christ died for us (Romans 5:8). May we learn from Jonah's story as we see ourselves as the Ninevites, unworthy of God's grace but chosen and redeemed by Him nonetheless.

> Jonah knew God was compassionate and loving and that He would extend His forgiveness to the evil people in Nineveh.

WHAT IS YOUR MAIN TAKEAWAY FROM THE STORY OF JONAH?

WHAT ASPECTS OF GOD'S CHARACTER DO YOU SEE THROUGHOUT THIS BOOK?

IN WHAT WAYS CAN YOU RELATE TO JONAH? IF YOU HAVE A HARD HEART TOWARD SOMEONE IN YOUR LIFE, SPEND SOME TIME IN CONFESSION BEFORE THE LORD.

2 Kings 15
2 Chronicles 26

AS WE RETURN TO THE NARRATIVE OF 2 KINGS AND 2 CHRONICLES, WE LEARN THAT AZARIAH, SON OF JUDAH'S KING AMAZIAH, WAS NEXT ON THE THRONE OF JUDAH.

Azariah, who is also called Uzziah in 2 Chronicles, began his reign at just sixteen years of age. The text states that he did what was right in the eyes of the Lord. He sought the Lord as the prophet Zechariah instructed him. Unfortunately, once he was strong, pride overcame him just as his father before him. He went into the temple to offer incense, which was a task specifically reserved for the priests. He was struck with leprosy as a consequence of his disobedience and lived the rest of his life with the disease.

Azariah's son, Jotham, was also a king described as doing right in the eyes of the Lord. He ordered his life in the way of the Lord, and God rewarded him for it. Yet, the cycle continues as Jotham neglects to take away the high places and the worship of false gods.

These chapters are a reminder for us to be obedient to the Lord above all, guarding our hearts and keeping ourselves pure before the Lord. These chapters chronicle kings who, though they had good aspects, also did things to displease the Lord. Jesus calls us to follow Him wholly and completely when He says, "Love the Lord your God with all your heart, with all your soul, with all your mind, and with all your strength" (Mark 12:30). Many kings neglected to do this, as they sought outward obedience while their hearts were far from God.

Amaziah, Azariah, and Jotham are all listed as kings who did what was right in the sight of the Lord, yet they struggled with idolatry, pride, and incomplete obedience. Thankfully, we do not have to look to human rulers to provide our ultimate security and hope. Jesus is our perfect example as the King of kings. He is the One we look to, and our allegiance is to His kingship. Through Christ, we learn to live and serve from a place of humble dependence, not prideful self-reliance. We will stumble and fail to do what is right, but Christ lived a perfect life on our behalf and died to cover our sins. We can look to our perfect King, knowing that we are secure in Him because of His finished work on the cross.

> Jesus is our perfect example as the King of kings.

HOW DID AZARIAH'S PRIDE IMPACT HIS REIGN? IF A BELIEVER IS PUFFED UP WITH PRIDE, WHAT DOES IT IMPLY ABOUT GOD'S ROLE IN HIS OR HER LIFE?

REFLECT ON MARK 12:30. WHAT ARE SOME WAYS YOU CAN LOVE GOD WITH ALL YOUR HEART, SOUL, MIND, AND STRENGTH?

IN WHAT WAYS DO THESE KINGS REFLECT GODLY WISDOM? IN WHAT WAYS DO THEY REFLECT WORLDLY WISDOM? HOW CAN YOU ENSURE THAT YOU SEEK COUNSEL FROM GOD OVER THE COUNSEL THAT THE WORLD OFFERS?

Amos 1–5

DURING THE REIGNS OF JEROBOAM II IN ISRAEL AND UZZIAH IN JUDAH (2 KINGS 14–15), GOD CALLED A SHEPHERD FROM JUDAH TO LEAVE HIS HOME AND PROPHESY TO HIS CHOSEN BUT WAYWARD PEOPLE.

The book of Amos begins with six judgment sermons on the neighboring nations surrounding Israel. But then the Lord's judgment turns from the nations toward His own people in Amos 2:4. God reminds Judah and Israel how He had delivered them, and He warned them of judgment if they did not turn back to Him. But they rebelled against God while relying upon their identity as His chosen people, hoping God would overlook their sin.

Chapters 3–4 reveal the reasons why the Lord was bringing judgment upon His chosen people. God's people were so blinded by their sin that Amos said they were unable to do what was right (Amos 3:10). God sent Amos to warn them and plead with them to repent. Though the people's hearts were far from Him, God sought to make a way to restore His people.

God had pleaded with them to return, but they would not. The people found their security in their military strength and their extravagant lifestyles. The Lord describes a series of hardships He brought upon His people to encourage them to return to Him, but they refused. These are similar to the plagues that the Lord carried out against Egypt in Exodus. This repeated pattern of their redemptive history should have caused them to repent and turn to the Lord. We see a plea for Israel to "seek the Lord and live" in Amos 5:5–6. But sadly, they ignored God's call to live an authentic faith. Thus, the chapter ends with God declaring that He is sending His people into exile.

Without Christ, our hearts are just the same as theirs. It is only because of Jesus that we can hate evil and love what is good. In Christ, we begin to desire justice and righteousness and hate injustice and oppression. The gospel gives us life and access to God through the death and resurrection of Christ. Through His atoning work on the cross, our desires and actions are transformed. Our lives completely change as our God leads us out of darkness and into His marvelous light (1 Peter 2:9).

> Though the people's hearts were far from Him, God sought to make a way to restore His people.

REFLECT ON AMOS 5:21–24. HOW DOES THIS INFORM OUR UNDERSTANDING OF WHAT GOD CARES MOST ABOUT?

IN WHAT WAYS ARE YOU TEMPTED TO IGNORE GOD'S CALL TO "SEEK THE LORD AND LIVE" IN FAVOR OF LIVING LIFE YOUR OWN WAY?

GOD SENT AMOS TO PREACH A MESSAGE OF REPENTANCE TO HIS PEOPLE. SPEND TIME REFLECTING ON YOUR OWN WALK WITH THE LORD AND HOW MUCH OF YOUR TIME IS SPENT IN CONFESSION AND REPENTANCE. LIST SOME WAYS YOU CAN GROW IN THIS AREA.

Amos 6–9

THE PEOPLE OF ISRAEL THOUGHT THEY HAD PLENTY OF EASE AND SECURITY IN THE PROMISES OF THE LORD.

They thought they could continue to sin and that God would overlook it. In Amos 6, the Lord responds to this way of thinking by destroying His own house—something Israel never thought He would do. He would use an enemy nation against them. Again, their history repeats itself as they would endure oppression as they did back in Egypt.

Amos 7 details a series of visions. With each vision, Amos intercedes and pleads for the Lord to relent. Amid our chronological journey through Scripture, we have seen God relent through the intercession of others (Genesis 18:16–33), but by the third vision, Amos understands. God's people have rejected Him, and He will no longer relent.

The chapter closes with a narrative about a priest named Amaziah. The priest tells King Jeroboam II that Amos is conspiring against the king. The priest rejects Amos's prophecies and seeks to expel him from the region. By Amaziah attempting to silence Amos, he was silencing the very message of God. This story reminds us that Jesus is our ultimate prophet and priest, for He declares the truth of God and offers Himself as the final and all-sufficient sacrifice for our sins. And like Amos, Jesus's message would not be well-received. But the gospel is a message that brings true hope and life to those who believe.

In the final two chapters, Amos warns of the bitter judgment that would come because the people refused to heed the Lord. He told the people that they would suffer immensely and no longer hear the Word of the Lord. No one would be able to hide from the Lord's sight (Amos 9:8). This should cause us to have a proper fear and respect for Him. No evil or injustice is unnoticed by Him, and He will have the final say.

The last five verses of Amos look forward to the day when all that is wrong will be made right. More importantly, these verses point to the One who would come as the Messiah for all of Israel and the world (Amos 9:11–15). Jesus is the promised Messiah. He has come with power to redeem even the most broken things, and through His blood, we are clothed in His righteousness. May we be people who seek Him above all else.

> The gospel is a message that brings true hope and life to those who believe.

**HOW WOULD YOU SUMMARIZE THE BOOK OF AMOS?
WHAT IS THE MAIN POINT OF THE PROPHET'S MESSAGE?**

**REFLECT ON JESUS AS OUR ULTIMATE PROPHET AND PRIEST.
HOW DOES THIS INFORM YOUR IDENTITY AS A CHILD OF GOD?**

**REFLECT ON AMOS 9:11–15 IN LIGHT OF THE ENTIRE BOOK.
WHAT DO THESE VERSES SHOW US ABOUT THE FAITHFULNESS OF GOD?**

Isaiah 1-4

AFTER AMOS'S PROPHECY, GOD CALLED ANOTHER PROPHET TO SPEAK TO HIS PEOPLE.

Isaiah prophesied in the eighth century during the reign of several kings (Isaiah 1:1). The name "Isaiah" means "salvation of the Lord," and as the Lord warns His people of coming judgment through the prophet Isaiah, He will fulfill the purpose behind the prophet's name. He will remind them again and again that the Lord alone is their salvation.

The book begins with God speaking to the prophet in a vision. At the time Isaiah prophesied, the nation of Israel has already split into two kingdoms: the northern kingdom (Israel) and the southern kingdom (Judah). Isaiah's prophecies are primarily for Judah, as the Lord longs to call the rebellious people back to Himself.

God's steadfast love was stronger than their sin. Though the record of their sin had declared them guilty, the Lord was ready to offer forgiveness. And He will do the same for us. Through the blood of Jesus, He removes our guilt and makes us white as snow (Isaiah 1:18, 1 John 1:7–9). Though we rebel, He is ready and waiting to forgive us (Psalm 86:5). Jesus is truth and justice perfectly coupled with love and grace. He is faithful to restore what is broken.

In chapter 2, Isaiah gives a promise full of a future hope as he describes the future city of God, which will draw people from all nations (Isaiah 2:1–4). The people of Judah were not living in such a way that pointed the nations to this future kingdom. They were living like all the other nations of the world, so the Lord promised them a day where He would act against them to humble them (Isaiah 2:12). God would not have this for His people. And while the judgment of the Lord would be upon His people, He would protect and uphold a faithful remnant, and the Messiah would still come from the line of Judah (Isaiah 3:10).

The people of God have drifted far from the Lord, but God brings hope to their desperate situation. In chapter 4, we read about the "Branch of the Lord," likely referring to the coming Messiah. How amazing that as Judah hears their judgment from God, He also emphasizes their future hope. In Christ, we share in the same future hope, and we look forward to the day when we will bow before the King and worship Him for all of eternity.

God's steadfast love was stronger than their sin.

ISAIAH 1:4–6 REVEALS JUDAH'S CONDITION WHEN THEY ABANDONED THE LORD. EXAMINE YOUR OWN HEART, AND CONFESS TO THE LORD THE WAYS YOU TURN YOUR BACK ON HIM.

THOUGH IDOL WORSHIP CAN SEEM OUTDATED, WE SIN IN SIMILAR WAYS WHEN WE EXALT CREATED THINGS OVER THE CREATOR. WHAT THINGS OR PEOPLE DO YOU TEND TO ELEVATE ABOVE GOD?

IN ISAIAH 4, GOD PRONOUNCES JUDGMENT, BUT HE ALSO PRONOUNCES RESTORATION. HOW HAVE YOU SEEN GOD RESTORE THE BROKENNESS IN YOUR OWN LIFE?

Isaiah 5-8

THROUGHOUT THE BOOK OF ISAIAH, WE READ ABOUT THE PEOPLE WHO WANDER AND THE LOVING GOD WHO STILL PURSUES THEM.

We identify with them as we also wander from the Lord and choose our sin over obedience to Him. Seeing God's people continually rebel—and seeing our own unfaithfulness in light of their rebellion—can be disheartening. But, as Isaiah continually reminds us, the Lord and His faithful love prove to be stronger.

Chapter 5 shows Israel's unfaithfulness up close as it reveals how far the people had drifted from God. Isaiah describes Israel as a vineyard that had not produced good fruit (Isaiah 5:1–7). Yet the Lord had constantly been faithful to His people, even though they were quick to wander from Him.

Isaiah 6 reveals a vision of the Lord on His throne in heaven. When Isaiah saw God's glory, he was humbled by his own sin. However, Isaiah was not left without hope, and neither are we. God is ready to redeem our brokenness for His glory. And, like Isaiah, we should be in awe of God's holiness, compelled to worship and serve Him. He is our hope, and He will always be with us.

Judah saw imminent destruction coming from Syria and Israel. Isaiah 7:2 says the people and king of Judah were fearful, shaking like trees in the wind. The king looked for help, not from God but from Assyria. And yet, amid King Ahaz's unbelief came the promise of a Messiah named Immanuel. Matthew 1:18–25 shows Jesus is this promised "Immanuel," which means, "God with us." As Judah saw their enemies closing in on them, God promised that He was with them, and this promise is ultimately carried out through the coming of Christ.

As the Lord describes the Assyrian invasion in Isaiah 8, He tenderly reminds Isaiah to trust in Him. Though the people will be full of fear, Isaiah and the remnant should not be afraid, for they know the Lord. His holiness is to be feared more than the Assyrians. Isaiah instructs those who are faithful to God to wait upon Him and put their hope in Him. While the wicked people in Judah will try to find comfort, Isaiah is told not to listen to them, for their hope is misplaced. This is a sober reminder for us to remember where our hope lies—not in our circumstances but in the powerful name of Jesus.

Like Isaiah, we should be in awe of God's holiness, compelled to worship and serve Him.

HOW DOES ISAIAH 6 INFORM YOUR RESPONSE TO GOD AND HIS HOLINESS?

REFLECT ON ISAIAH 7:9. WHAT DOES IT LOOK LIKE TO STAND FIRM IN YOUR FAITH? HOW DOES STANDING FIRM INFORM HOW YOU FACE DIFFICULT SITUATIONS?

HOW DOES GOD USE WATER AS A WAY TO DESCRIBE JUDAH'S REJECTION OF HIM AND THEIR IMPENDING JUDGMENT (ISAIAH 8:5–10)?

2 Chronicles 27–28
2 Kings 16–17

SECOND CHRONICLES 27 IS A BRIEF CHAPTER THAT PICKS BACK UP WITH JOTHAM AS KING OF JUDAH.

Jotham was considered to be a good king overall. He only reigned for sixteen years, but Matthew includes Jotham in the genealogy of Jesus in his gospel account, showing the importance of his reign (Matthew 1:9).

In 2 Kings 16 and 2 Chronicles 28, we meet the next king: King Ahaz. Remember, this is the king that Isaiah was sent to as he shared God's message of judgment (Isaiah 7). This evil king in Judah did not do what was right in God's eyes. Ahaz even engaged in the horrific act of child sacrifice, killing his own son as an offering to a false god. His sin would bring great consequences and military defeat.

These chapters provide a turning point in Israel's history. Though God remained true to His nature (Exodus 34:6–7), His people still did not listen. They wanted to do things their own way. God's people embraced syncretism, which was a cultural form of religion where they mixed up various beliefs and practices. As we continue to read through the Israelites' history, it seems that they wanted to say that they feared the Lord but not enough to give up their idols.

In His great love and mercy, God sent prophet after prophet to warn His people to turn from their sin and back toward God, but they refused to listen. The children of Israel were stubborn, did not obey God's commands, ran after false gods, and followed the nations around them. Things were bad in Judah and even worse in Israel. In 2 Kings 17, we witness the downfall of the northern kingdom of Israel. After all that the Lord had done for them, God's people continued to rebel, and now they would face exile from their homeland.

As they were led into exile, the people were scattered among different regions in Assyria to ensure a low chance of rebellion while in captivity. It seemed that all hope was lost. But this is not the end of their story. God's faithfulness would greatly outweigh the people's unfaithfulness. We serve a covenant-keeping God. Jesus came not to abolish the Law but to fulfill it (Matthew 5:17), and He did so on our behalf. We are not exiled for our sin. Instead, we are brought near and given the title "child of God" (1 John 3:1).

> We are not exiled for our sin. Instead, we are brought near and given the title "child of God."

GENERATION AFTER GENERATION, GOD HAD WARNED OF EXILE THROUGH HIS LAW AND THROUGH HIS PROPHETS. HE PROVIDED OPPORTUNITIES FOR HIS PEOPLE TO REPENT AND TURN BACK TO HIM. HOW DOES THIS INFORM HOW YOU VIEW GOD'S CHARACTER AS YOU READ THE OLD TESTAMENT?

THOUGH WE DO NOT WORSHIP ACTUAL IDOLS OR FALSE GODS, THERE IS A LOT IN OUR SOCIETY TODAY THAT IS WORSHIPED AND IDOLIZED. HOW DOES YOUR LIFE REFLECT WORSHIP OF CHRIST, RATHER THAN WORSHIP OF WORLDLY POSSESSIONS OR STATUS?

WHO, OR WHAT, IN YOUR LIFE CHALLENGES YOU TO SEEK OBEDIENCE AND REPENTANCE OVER SIN?

2 Chronicles 27–28, 2 Kings 16–17

Micah 1-7

LIKE MANY OF THE OTHER PROPHETS, MICAH WARNED GOD'S PEOPLE OF THE IMPENDING JUDGMENT FOR THEIR SIN,

but he also pointed toward the future restoration of the repentant. Micah prophesied during the reigns of Judah's kings Jotham, Ahaz, and Hezekiah (Micah 1:1).

Micah opens each of his three messages with a command for the people to "hear" or "listen," and he laments over their unwillingness to repent. In chapter 2, Micah specifically calls out those who oppressed and seized the property of others. But, though His rebellious people would be exiled, the Lord would gather His faithful remnant and shepherd them (Micah 2:12). Micah 3, however, shows that leaders were unconcerned about the sin of the nation because they were God's chosen people. They thought they were protected from God's punishment. They took advantage of God's grace. Likewise, professing Christians must not take advantage of God's patience (Romans 2:4). Sin must not be our friend. It will wreak havoc on our lives and draw us away from spiritual growth and joy in the Lord.

Micah's message brings promises of hope that follow the warnings of judgment. Chapter 4 reveals that Jerusalem would be restored, and the nations would come to learn the ways of the Lord. This is a picture of the New Jerusalem, our heavenly home, with Jesus reigning as King. Micah 5:1–5 shows that the Messiah would come from Bethlehem to deliver His people and shepherd the nation. This is fulfilled by Christ, who would be unlike any other king the world had ever known or will ever know—this King would bring everlasting peace.

The last message of Micah is a reminder of what God desires from sinners. Chapter 6 begins with the Lord bringing "a case" against His people for their sins. In the midst of His judgment, the Lord tells His people what He requires of them in Micah 6:8. This is a depiction of the perfect life of Christ. Jesus perfectly embodies justice, kindness, and humility. He sanctifies us and leads us into this kind of life as well. Micah 6 reveals that the Israelites will face desolation for their sins. Yet the book of Micah ends with a declaration about our faithful God. Though His people would see destruction and exile, God would deliver them and bring them home. He would forgive them of their sins and cast their sins "into the depths of the sea" (Micah 7:19). We can place our hope in our God and be confident that He will never fail His people.

> Though His people would see destruction and exile, God would deliver them and bring them home.

HOW WOULD YOU SUMMARIZE THE MAIN POINT OF THE BOOK OF MICAH?

WHAT HOPE IS PROVIDED TO GOD'S PEOPLE THROUGHOUT THIS BOOK?
HOW DOES THIS REMIND YOU OF YOUR ETERNAL HOPE?

MEDITATE ON MICAH 6:8. HOW CAN YOU PRACTICALLY APPLY THIS VERSE IN YOUR OWN LIFE?

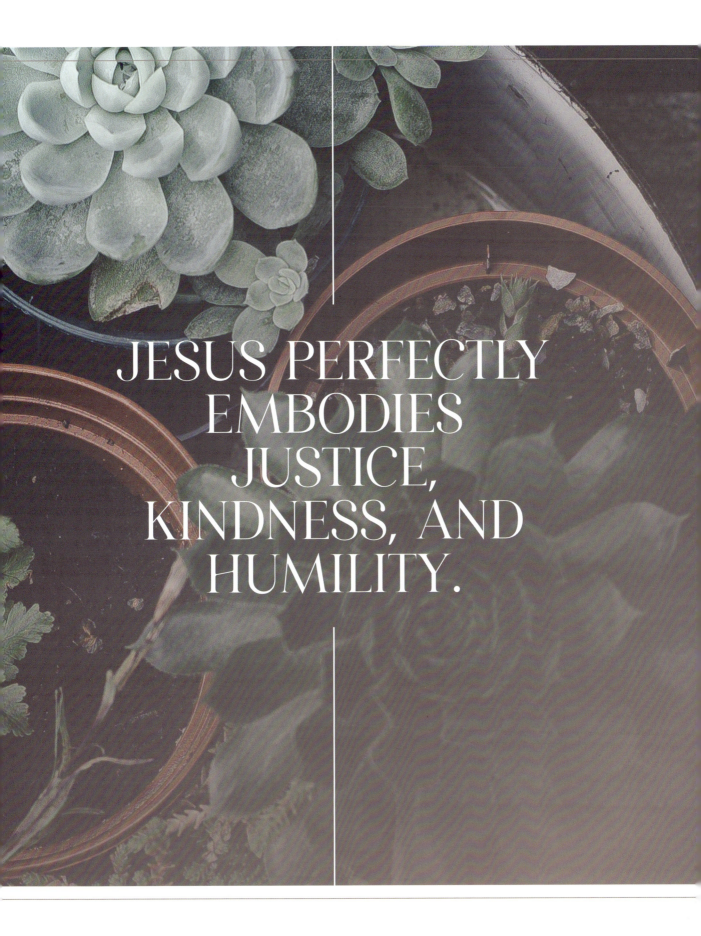

2 Chronicles 29–31
2 Kings 18:1–8
Psalm 48

THESE PASSAGES IN 2 CHRONICLES AND 2 KINGS INTRODUCE US TO A DIFFERENT KIND OF KING.

Hezekiah, the son of Ahaz, was one of the best kings that Judah would ever know. He did what was right in the eyes of the Lord and is described as being a king like David (2 Kings 18:3, 2 Chronicles 29:2). He cleansed the temple, restored the temple worship, and brought the people together to celebrate the Passover for the first time in a long time. The high places were torn down, and the evil that Ahaz instituted was systematically dismantled.

Under Hezekiah, the people of God were called to repentance. They were urged to turn their hearts back to their covenant God, yield to Him, come to His sanctuary, and serve Him alone. The people were reminded that the Lord is gracious and merciful and would not turn from them if they returned to Him. The result was great joy in Jerusalem and the Lord hearing the prayers of His people.

Hezekiah grows our longing for a better king, King Jesus. He is gracious and merciful to His people. Despite our stubbornness and rebellion, God never stops pursuing His own. God's covenant promises are extended to us only through Jesus Christ. It is in Him that we can fully comprehend the grace and mercy of God. And it is through Him that we find joy everlasting. The goodness of Jesus should turn our hearts to worship, just as it did in Judah so many years ago. Grace and mercy are found in Him alone.

As we read about Judah's renewal under Hezekiah, we also reflect on the words of the psalmist in Psalm 48 as he declares that Judah rejoices because of the Lord's judgments (Psalm 48:11). This stands in stark contrast to the cycle of kings that has come through Israel and Judah, many of them seeking their own glory rather than God's. Not only that, but this psalm acts as a reminder that His goodness is to be proclaimed throughout the generations (Psalm 48:12–14). While the psalmist is speaking of the city of Jerusalem in Psalm 48, his words give us a glimpse into the New Jerusalem where God will dwell with His people from all different tribes, tongues, and nations (Revelation 21). We look forward to that day when God will wipe away every tear and make all things new.

> Hezekiah grows our longing for a better king, King Jesus.

HOW HAS YOUR UNDERSTANDING OF ISRAEL'S HISTORY DEEPENED BY READING THE KINGS AND PROPHETS CHRONOLOGICALLY?

HOW WAS HEZEKIAH DIFFERENT FROM PREVIOUS KINGS? HOW DOES THIS EARTHLY KING POINT US TO OUR ETERNAL KING JESUS?

REFLECT ON PSALM 48:12–14. WHAT ARE THINGS IN YOUR LIFE THAT YOU CAN POINT TO SO THAT YOU CAN TELL FUTURE GENERATIONS OF GOD'S GOODNESS?

Isaiah 9–12

DESPITE THE REIGN OF HEZEKIAH, WHO WE LEARNED YESTERDAY WAS A GOOD KING OVERALL, THE PEOPLE WERE STILL SINFUL, AND THEY WOULD ONCE AGAIN BE RULED BY EVIL LEADERS AND FACE THE CONSEQUENCES OF THEIR ACTIONS IN THE YEARS TO COME.

In this seemingly hopeless moment in Judah's history, another promise brings hope. Despite their sin, God's commitment to be with His people remains. In Isaiah 9, we read Isaiah's prophecy of the promised Immanuel, who will bring light to the darkness and lift the burden that the people carried. When He comes, He will be their "Wonderful Counselor, Mighty God, Eternal Father, Prince of Peace" (Isaiah 9:6). He will bring peace between God and man, and He will give His peace to the hearts of all those who follow Him. War and destruction will not last forever. Soon, Assyria will take God's people into exile. However, while the king of Assyria may boast and proclaim his power and might over the Israelites for a time, he is only a tool in the Lord's hands to carry out His sovereign plan (Isaiah 10:12–15). Just like the Lord brought Egypt to ruin, so would be the fate of Assyria.

Isaiah 11 shows again how God will keep His promises in the coming of the Messiah. Jesus fulfills every word of this as the "root of Jesse," allowing those who call on His name to bear good fruit. During Jesus's baptism, the Holy Spirit descended upon Him (Matthew 3:13–17), fulfilling the words of Isaiah 11:2, "The Spirit of the Lord will rest on Him." In His first coming, Jesus walked in understanding and fear of His heavenly Father. He brought the peace and love of God to a broken world in chaos. Much of Isaiah 11 is fulfilled in Christ's first coming, but some of it will come to completion in His second coming when the world will be forever free from the curse of sin (1 Corinthians 15:50–58).

Isaiah 12 presents a song of praise as the response God's people will have on that day. It also shows us the posture that our hearts should have even now. Our hearts should overflow with overwhelming gratitude and praise for who God is and all He has done for us. While the people of Judah will be tempted to question and reject God for His judgment, He has promised that they will see Him as their salvation. There is a day coming when the world will finally bow to God as Creator, and His people will be in His presence forever.

Despite their sin, God's commitment to be with His people remains.

REFLECT ON THE NAMES ISAIAH USES TO REFER TO THE LORD (ISAIAH 9:6, 10:20).
WHAT DO WE LEARN ABOUT GOD'S CHARACTER FROM THESE NAMES?

WHAT ARE SOME OF THE THINGS YOU LEARNED FROM THESE PROPHECIES OF A COMING MESSIAH?

THROUGHOUT SCRIPTURE, GOD CONTINUALLY PROMISES THE REDEMPTION OF HIS PEOPLE.
REFLECT ON YOUR OWN STORY OF HOW GOD HAS REDEEMED YOU.
THANK HIM FOR THE WAYS HE HAS BROUGHT GOD'S PEACE AND LOVE TO YOUR BROKENNESS.

Isaiah 13–17

WHILE THE BOOK OF ISAIAH OPENS WITH GOD'S JUDGMENT ON HIS PEOPLE FOR THEIR SIN, ISAIAH 13 FOCUSES ON GOD'S JUDGMENT ON BABYLON, THE PEOPLE WHO WILL CARRY JUDAH INTO EXILE.

The Lord will have His day of wrath against the Babylonians, but there is also a day coming when He will have judgment over all of the earth (Isaiah 13:9–11). When Jesus comes back to the earth to reign, He will bring justice against those who have opposed God, and He will deliver His people from the curse of sin forever.

After the judgment on Babylon, God promises hope and deliverance for Judah. He will have compassion on them and bring them home (Isaiah 14:1). Not only that, but His people will have victory over their captors. Later in the chapter, Isaiah describes Babylon's king, who has fallen after trying to place himself in equal standing with the Lord (Isaiah 14:12–16). Followers of Jesus will one day sing a song of triumph when the ultimate enemy of God is defeated, and sin and death are no more (Revelation 19:1–3, 21:4). We will be free as we worship God for all of eternity.

Isaiah chapters 15–16 contain the Lord's judgment against the nation of Moab. The Moabites were distant relatives to the Israelites (Genesis 19:30–38), which may explain the empathy toward Moab in Isaiah 15:5. God does not delight in judgment, but He disciplines for the good of His creation and the glory of His name. He will always do what is just and right. Isaiah 16:3–4 is from the perspective of the Moabites, asking for shelter and refuge. In response to Moab's need for security, a loving and faithful king is promised. The Messiah King is promised in this passage. He will welcome the nations, and His reign will be characterized by His love and faithfulness (Isaiah 16:5).

In Isaiah 17, God pronounces judgments on Damascus and Israel, who have joined forces against Judah. Judgment will ultimately lead the people to a day when they will look to the Lord for deliverance, for their man-made idols and gods will not be able to save them (Isaiah 17:7–8). These verses remind us to focus our hearts on the Lord alone instead of worshiping things of this world. Nothing in this world is more precious than the Lord Himself — the giver of all good gifts.

We will be free as we worship God for all of eternity.

REFLECT ON ISAIAH 14:1–2. HOW DOES GOD DISPLAY HIS COMPASSION TOWARD YOU?

HOW DO VERSES LIKE ISAIAH 14:24–27 HELP YOU REFLECT ON GOD'S SOVEREIGNTY, BOTH IN ISRAEL'S HISTORY AND IN YOUR OWN LIFE?

HOW DO THESE CHAPTERS INFORM YOUR UNDERSTANDING OF GOD'S HOLINESS AND THE NEED FOR JUSTICE?

Isaiah 18–22

ISAIAH'S MESSAGE OF WOE AND JUDGMENT CONTINUES AS HE SHARES THE WORD OF THE LORD WITH OTHER NATIONS.

But in Isaiah 18, there is a brief glimmer of hope for one nation. God tells Judah to send messengers to the people of Cush—the Ethiopians. The Lord was making a way for the Cushites to worship and know Him. God would use His people's exile and deliverance to draw the nations to Himself. This same pattern would continue as Jesus came to draw all people to Himself and make every tribe, tongue, and nation a part of God's family.

In chapter 19, Egypt receives a prophecy of judgment from the Lord. Egypt, like Babylon, became a representative for all the enemies of God and His people. God would bring judgment on this nation that had oppressed His people, but He would also extend mercy. Intertwined in this message of judgment is one of hope for both Egypt and Assyria as God promised they would one day be blessed by Israel, and there would be an alliance between them. God not only restored His chosen people, but through Jesus, He restored all the nations of the world.

Isaiah 20 is brief but powerful. God's people chose to seek aid from Egypt and Cush instead of pleading with Him for deliverance from Assyria. So Isaiah is instructed to do the unthinkable to show how Egypt and Cush would be judged for this alliance: walk around completely naked for three years. These nations would be exiled, and they would be naked as they left.

Chapter 21 declares the Lord's judgment of Babylon. The Babylonians thought their city was impenetrable, but they would be conquered and slaughtered by the Persians and Medes as they ate and drank in false security. Babylon also represents the sinful nations and people that exist today. Judgment has been prophesied and is coming. Jesus is the only hope for salvation!

In chapter 22, God turns His message of judgment toward the northern kingdom of Israel. This chapter is heartbreaking as it shows God's chosen people had become like the world. They were meant to be different. They were meant to reflect the Lord. The Lord desired their repentance, but instead, they indulged in worldly pleasures, becoming hardened in their sin. Israel, unlike the other nations, had access to God's truth and wisdom, yet they chose to reject Him. Sadly, people still reject Him today. Without Jesus, those who live in darkness will share the same fate as the exiled Israelites.

Jesus is the only hope for salvation!

READ GENESIS 12:3. HOW DOES ISAIAH 18–19 DISPLAY FULFILLMENT OF GOD'S COVENANT TO ABRAHAM? HOW DOES JESUS BRING COMPLETE FULFILLMENT? (READ ROMANS 1:16 FOR HELP ANSWERING THIS QUESTION.)

ISAIAH WAS WILLING TO DO ALL THE LORD COMMANDED HIM TO DO, EVEN PROPHESY WHILE NAKED. ARE YOU WILLING TO BE HUMILIATED OR SUFFER FOR THE SAKE OF THE GOSPEL? READ 1 PETER 4:12–14 FOR ENCOURAGEMENT, AND RECORD A PRAYER ASKING GOD TO GIVE YOU A WILLING HEART.

HOW DO CHRISTIANS INCREASINGLY LOOK LIKE THE WORLD? WHAT PRACTICAL STEPS CAN YOU TAKE TO LOOK MORE LIKE CHRIST AND LESS LIKE THE WORLD?

Isaiah 18–22

Isaiah 23–27

JUDGMENT CONTINUES FOR THE NATIONS OF THE WORLD AS WE READ ISAIAH'S PRONOUNCEMENT AGAINST TYRE IN ISAIAH 23.

Tyre was a very wealthy and powerful trading city in the Mediterranean. Tyre represents the lust and greed for worldly possessions, power, and wealth. The Lord promises in Isaiah 23:18 that the wealth of Tyre will eventually be inherited by God's people. In Christ, the humble will inherit the earth, not those who are greedy (Matthew 5:5). When we follow Jesus, our treasure is in His heavenly kingdom.

Isaiah 24–27 contains a poetic apocalyptic prophecy sometimes referred to as Isaiah's Apocalypse. This prophetic message begins in chapter 24 as a judgment of the entire world. Even though this prophecy gives believers hope, it should stir us to action for the sake of the gospel. While Christians have great hope, there will be many who will be separated from Christ forever. Followers of Christ must be on mission to share Jesus with the world. We look forward to the day when God and man will dwell together again.

Isaiah 25 continues this poetic prophecy. While God will judge the sin of the world, this chapter mainly displays the Lord's goodness and provision through His redemptive plan for all mankind. Even before God sent Christ to die for our sins, He provided a way for all people to know Him through the message of Isaiah. Jesus destroyed "the burial shroud" of sin (Isaiah 25:7). Jesus "swallowed up death once and for all" through His perfect life, atoning death, and glorious resurrection (Isaiah 25:8).

Isaiah's message is directed to Judah in chapter 26. God will show Judah how to endure as they await the promises of the Messiah to come. Though the people will be exiled because of judgment, they must remember their true home is God's coming city. Isaiah says that if they keep their minds fixed on God, He will keep them in "perfect peace" (Isaiah 26:3). This peace is rooted in the knowledge that the Lord has accomplished salvation for them—past, present, and future.

Chapter 27 completes this apocalyptic poem with a metaphor of a vineyard. This metaphor displays how the Lord watches over, nurtures, and protects Israel. He also offers peace to those who have once been at enmity with Him. God will provide a rescuer. Through this tiny nation, all nations will be blessed by Jesus. Our God redeems us. He uses even our weakness for His glory. He did it for Israel, and He can certainly do it for us as well.

> When we follow Jesus, our treasure is in His heavenly kingdom.

WHAT DO YOU LOOK FORWARD TO THE MOST WHEN GOD MAKES ALL THINGS NEW AND WE DWELL WITH HIM FOREVER IN THE NEW HEAVEN AND NEW EARTH, AS DESCRIBED IN REVELATION 21:1–3?

ISAIAH 26:3 SAYS, "YOU WILL KEEP THE MIND THAT IS DEPENDENT ON YOU IN PERFECT PEACE, FOR IT IS TRUSTING IN YOU." IN WHAT WAYS CAN YOU KEEP YOUR MIND DEPENDENT ON THE LORD SO YOU CAN HAVE PEACE EVEN IN A CHAOTIC WORLD?

READ JOHN 15:1–5. HOW DOES JESUS FULFILL THE METAPHOR OF THE VINEYARD?

Hosea 1–7

THE PROPHETIC MINISTRIES OF ISAIAH AND HOSEA HAD SOME OVERLAP.

While Isaiah mostly prophesied to Judah, Hosea's message from the Lord was to Israel, or Ephraim, the northern kingdom. Hosea prophesied before the fall of Israel, and his life was a living sermon of God's steadfast and unfailing love. God called Hosea to marry a prostitute named Gomer. She would be unfaithful to him multiple times. Hosea's marriage to Gomer was symbolic of the Lord's relationship with Israel. God chose Israel and gave Himself to them as a faithful husband, but they prostituted themselves to foreign gods. Hosea and Gomer's children had symbolic names, which announced God's judgment on His people.

In chapter 2, God pleads with His people to turn from their sins, but they ignore His warnings. God exiles Israel so that they will see the foolishness of their idol worship and realize that He alone is their hope. His punishment of Israel would ultimately bring their salvation. The Lord would again speak tender words to Israel and restore their covenant relationship. God commanded Hosea to act out this covenant relationship by seeking out his unfaithful wife, buying her back from adultery, and promising her restoration (Hosea 3). In the same way, God would return His people to the land from their exile and restore them. Complete restoration for all people finds its consummation in Christ.

Though Hosea would buy Gomer back, she would continue in her promiscuity. Israel did the same. Hosea 4–5 presents God's case against Israel and their coming punishment. Israel neglected the Lord and sought the gods, pleasure, and wealth of the pagan nations around them. Their self-sufficiency and rebellion against the Lord would bring destruction and exile from the very nation from which they sought help. Assyria would destroy Israel, and the Lord would depart from His people.

Hosea pleads with the people to return to the Lord in chapter 6. If the people returned to God, He would heal them, revive them, and renew their relationship. But the people were just like their ancestor, Adam, who sinned against the Lord in the garden of Eden. Hosea 7 further exposes Israel's evil and God's woe against them. They would fall by the sword and be ridiculed among the nations. The arrogance of the people would be their downfall as they preferred the false comforts of the world to the lasting and enduring love of the Lord. We must heed these same warnings and remember nothing compares to a life wholly devoted to Christ.

His punishment of Israel would ultimately bring their salvation.

WHAT IDOLS IN YOUR LIFE HAVE TAKEN YOU AWAY FROM THE LORD? HOW HAVE THEY HINDERED YOUR TIME IN THE WORD OR TIME SPENT IN A GOSPEL-CENTERED COMMUNITY?

READ HOSEA 6:3. DO YOU STRIVE TO KNOW THE LORD? HOW HAS GOD SHOWN HIS STEADFAST LOVE IN YOUR LIFE, EVEN WHEN YOU SEEK AFTER OTHER THINGS? HOW HAS HE DRAWN YOU BACK?

HOW DOES JESUS BRING ULTIMATE RESTORATION TO OUR HEARTS? HOW IS HE THE ONLY ONE WHO WILL SATISFY OUR HEARTS?

Hosea 8-14

THE MANY REASONS FOR ISRAEL'S FUTURE EXILE CONTINUE IN HOSEA 8.

As the people rejected God and lived in darkness, they hypocritically tried to claim that they knew Him, but their actions displayed the opposite. Instead of worshiping God, they set up idols and kings to replace Him. They patterned their lives after the surrounding nations and became just like them.

Hosea shows the people the result of living in rebellion to God in chapter 9. Because they forsook the Lord and prostituted themselves to other gods and nations, they would not remain in the Lord's land, and they would face destruction. God rejected them as they have rejected Him. In chapter 10, Israel is compared to an unfaithful and unfruitful vine. They have "plowed wickedness and reaped injustice" (Hosea 10:13). Israel's "extreme evil" would bring their destruction (Hosea 10:15).

In chapter 11, we see a brief reprieve from God's pronouncement of judgment. The Lord had a great love for His people, and He displays it through a tender poem about a father's love for his child. Despite their rejection and rebellion against Him, the Lord could not bear the thought of separation from Israel. He was full of compassion and love for them. God's love and kindness should have led Israel to repentance, but they continued to reject Him. Israel's pattern of sin occurred repeatedly throughout their history. Hosea reminds them of their redemptive history in chapter 12. Despite their sinful patterns, God sought His people and blessed them with covenants and promises. God had been with them from the beginning, and his discipline would bring them back in the future.

The final two chapters of Hosea call the people to remember who God is and how He had always been with them and for them. Unlike man-made idols and kings, God receives, restores, and revives His people. We must remember this too! Pausing to consider how God has restored us and who He is helps us to be filled with gratitude and love for Him. This, in turn, keeps us from drifting and chasing after the idols of this world. Though we wander, God calls us back to Himself. Jesus brings us home to the Father and restores all things.

> Despite their sinful patterns, God sought His people and blessed them with covenants and promises.

IN WHAT WAYS ARE YOU TEMPTED TO CLAIM BELIEF IN THE GOSPEL BUT THEN LIVE LIKE THE WORLD? WHAT WARNINGS DO YOU FIND IN 1 JOHN 2:15–17.

READ TITUS 3:4–7. HOW HAS GOD SHOWN US KINDNESS AND RESTORATION?

WHAT CAN YOU LEARN FROM ISRAEL'S HISTORY AND PATTERN OF SIN? HOW DOES HOSEA'S MESSAGE HELP YOU FOLLOW THE LORD AND NOT SEEK THE THINGS OF THIS WORLD?

Isaiah 28–31

AFTER STUDYING HOSEA, WE RETURN TO ISAIAH TO FIND THE LORD DIRECTING HIS ATTENTION FROM JUDAH TO THE NORTHERN KINGDOM OF ISRAEL, ALSO KNOWN AS SAMARIA, IN CHAPTER 28.

Just as we saw in Hosea, Israel would face judgment for their rejection of the Lord, and their destruction was a warning to the people of Judah in the southern kingdom. The northern kingdom had become proud and drunk with the pleasure of the world. They forgot the Lord and the treasure of being His children. Even the priests and prophets behaved wickedly and treated the Lord's words with contempt, so the Lord promised their coming judgment at the hands of the Assyrians. Israel's judgment was meant to give Judah a clear example of their sin, as Isaiah warns them in the following chapters.

Isaiah shifts to a message of woe for Jerusalem and Judah in chapter 29. The people of Judah honored God with lip service, but their hearts were cold toward Him (Isaiah 29:13). Jesus references this verse while speaking to the Pharisee in Matthew 15:7–8 which says, "Hypocrites! Isaiah prophesied correctly about you when he said: This people honors me with their lips, but their heart is far from me." The Lord desires more than just words. He desires a heart that is completely surrendered to Him. Cold hearts were a problem for Judah just as much as they were a problem for the Pharisees, and they remain a problem for us today. We must repent and submit ourselves to the Lord.

Chapters 30–31 show us that instead of repentance, Judah was quick to place their faith in the things that they could see. In Exodus, it was a golden calf, and here in Isaiah, it was the nation of Egypt. Judah saw Assyria conquer nation after nation, including the northern kingdom. Their fear led them to trust in visible signs of strength, such as horses and chariots. Isaiah tells the people that the Lord can demolish any of Judah's enemies with a raised hand. He is a growling lion and a tender bird protecting His children (Isaiah 31:4–5). Judah needs only to repent and return to the Lord, and He would act on their behalf.

Judah sought security from armies and military powers, not remembering their strength came from the Lord alone. God shows us through Isaiah that our preoccupation with the things of this world and even our self-sufficiency prevents us from seeing His provision. We must be cautious about trusting the fleeting things of this world. It is the Lord who will remain forever.

> The Lord desires more than just words. He desires a heart that is completely surrendered to Him.

ACCORDING TO PSALM 51:17, WHAT KIND OF HEART DOES THE LORD DESIRE?
HOW HAD JUDAH FAILED IN THIS?

IN WHAT AREAS OF YOUR LIFE DO YOU STRUGGLE WITH SELF-SUFFICIENCY? HOW CAN YOU PRACTICE GIVING THOSE AREAS OF YOUR LIFE TO THE LORD AND ALLOWING HIM TO WORK ON YOUR BEHALF?

READ ISAIAH 30:18. HOW HAS THE LORD SHOWN YOU MERCY AND COMPASSION?
WHY ARE BELIEVERS HAPPIEST WHEN THEY WAIT ON HIM?

Isaiah 28–31

Isaiah 32–35
Psalm 46

AT THE BEGINNING OF CHAPTER 32, ISAIAH CONTRASTS A FOOLISH AND A RIGHTEOUS KING.

This prophecy was likely given during the reign of King Ahaz, who was one of the wicked kings of Judah. His son, Hezekiah, would be a near fulfillment of this prophecy of a king reigning in righteousness. But ultimately, this prophecy finds complete fulfillment in Jesus, the true King of righteousness. Isaiah placed great emphasis on the peace that accompanies righteousness. Jesus is our righteousness, and He is our peace.

Chapter 33 begins with a promise of Assyria's destruction. Judah had long feared an Assyrian invasion and had aligned themselves with nations they felt could defend them. God warned them to trust in Him alone, and Judah finally turned to the Lord for deliverance. But not before Judah had lost its fortified cities to the Assyrians. God preserved Jerusalem and saved His people once again. In the final verses of chapter 33, the Lord gives the people of Judah the gospel. He tells them of the righteous One, who is Christ. Jesus gives His people His righteousness, so they can dwell with God and be in His presence.

Our merciful God is also a God of justice. Isaiah 34 shows us the fate of those who reject God. While the prophecy finds its first fulfillment in nations who come against Israel, it ultimately points to the judgment of everyone who turns their back on the Lord. "Edom" refers to the descendants of Esau, the older brother of Jacob. However, Edom is often used to describe those who will never believe in Jesus for salvation. This passage reminds us that judgment is coming. We must share the gospel with urgency!

Though judgment will come, Isaiah 35 reminds us that the redeemed will one day sing a jubilant song. Isaiah's song promises a remnant, or a small group of exiles, would return to Judah one day, but more importantly, Jesus will come again and make all things new. The earth will be filled with the Lord's glory. Psalm 46 has a similar message. Until the end comes, we find our refuge and security in Christ. This psalm also points to the eternal city of God, where Jesus will reign forever. After all of the kingdoms of the earth fall away, only the kingdom of God will remain. Isaiah and the psalmist knew the Lord was with His people in spirit, but one day we will physically be in His presence in eternity.

Jesus gives His people His righteousness, so they can dwell with God and be in His presence.

HOW DO YOU SEE GOD'S PATIENCE ON DISPLAY IN THESE CHAPTERS?
HOW HAS HE BEEN PATIENT WITH YOU?

ISAIAH 34 REMINDS US THAT JUDGMENT WILL COME. DO YOU SHARE THE GOSPEL WITH URGENCY?
HOW CAN YOU MAKE SHARING THE GOSPEL PART OF YOUR DAILY LIFE?

PSALM 46:11 SAYS, "THE LORD OF ARMIES IS WITH US; THE GOD OF JACOB IS OUR STRONGHOLD."
HOW HAVE YOU CLEARLY SEEN THIS THROUGHOUT YOUR READING OF SCRIPTURE THUS FAR?
WHAT MAJOR EVENTS STAND OUT TO SHOWCASE GOD'S GREAT FAITHFULNESS?

Isaiah 32–35, Psalm 46

2 Chronicles 32
2 Kings 18:9–37,
Isaiah 36, Psalm 80

Editor's Note: In this entry, we look at one of the Psalms of Asaph. As we continue our chronological journey through Scripture, it is important to note that we cannot date this psalm to this time period with absolute certainty. That said, the ideas expressed in this psalm are relevant to what is happening in 2 Chronicles 32, 2 Kings 18:9–37, and Isaiah 36, which is why we have placed it here.

ISAIAH 36 SHIFTS FROM PROPHECY TO A HISTORICAL NARRATIVE.

Included in this narrative are the events that are also found in 2 Chronicles 32 and 2 Kings 18:9–37. These chapters recount the enmity between Assyria and Judah. The northern kingdom—also referred to as Israel, Samaria, and Ephraim by various prophets—had been destroyed and taken into exile. Hezekiah, a good king, now sits on the throne of Judah, which is the southern kingdom. King Sennacherib of Assyria invaded the fortified cities of Judah and overtook them. King Hezekiah attempted to buy off Sennacherib in order to save Judah from seemingly inevitable annihilation, but Sennacherib broke his word after receiving the money he demanded.

Sennacherib sent his royal spokesman—whom some Bible translations identify as Rabshakeh or simply his "field commander"—and a great army to the last standing city of Judah, which was Jerusalem. As this great army approached Jerusalem, Hezekiah encouraged the people not to fear and to trust in the Lord their God, who would be with them every step of the way. He also fortified the city and set military commanders over the people as they prepared to fight. Rabshakeh came against Hezekiah and the Lord with wicked and evil words and called all of the people of Judah to rely on Assyria instead of their God and king. Hezekiah and Isaiah prayed to the Lord for deliverance. The Lord answered and sent an angel who annihilated the Assyrian army, and King Sennacherib returned home in disgrace. Upon his return home, he was struck down by his own children. The Lord avenged the people of Judah just as He promised.

These events tie into Psalm 80, which is a psalm of Asaph that reminds us that the Lord is the Shepherd of Israel. Asaph pleads for the Lord's restoration, just as Hezekiah and Isaiah did for Jerusalem. The attacks of Rabshakeh are no different than Satan's attacks today. Even though in certain situations it may seem that all is lost, we must believe that the Lord is our deliverer. There is no power greater than Him, no matter how threatening someone may appear. When Satan attacks us with words of deception, we should be like the officials from Hezekiah's government who refused to answer.

In Psalm 80:19, Asaph writes, "Restore us, Lord, God of Armies; make your face shine on us, so that we may be saved." Likewise, we are reminded that salvation comes from the Lord alone. Just as the Lord saved Judah from Sennacherib, He would save all people through Jesus. No matter what the enemy may throw at us, Jesus brings restoration and hope.

HEZEKIAH TRIED TO PAY OFF SENNACHERIB BEFORE HE TURNED TO THE LORD FOR HELP.
IN WHAT WAYS HAVE YOU TRIED TO SOLVE A PROBLEM OR SITUATION IN YOUR OWN STRENGTH,
WITHOUT THE HELP OR INSTRUCTION OF THE LORD?

HOW DO THE PRAYERS OF HEZEKIAH AND ISAIAH ENCOURAGE YOU TO PRAY?
HOW HAVE YOU SEEN THE LORD ANSWER YOUR OWN PRAYERS?

HOW DOES GOD'S HAND OF MERCY THROUGHOUT HISTORY AND ACROSS THE PAGES
OF SCRIPTURE ENCOURAGE YOU?

2 Chronicles 32, 2 Kings 18:9–37, Isaiah 36, Psalm 80

2 Kings 19–20
Isaiah 37–39
Psalm 76

OUR READING YESTERDAY GAVE US AN OVERVIEW OF SENNACHERIB'S ATTEMPTED INVASION OF JUDAH.

Today, we get to zoom in and read more details about the prayer of Hezekiah and Isaiah's response concerning deliverance. Both 2 Kings 19–20 and Isaiah 37–39 detail the account of these prayers, Sennacherib's fall, Hezekiah's illness, and his final folly. Hezekiah serves as a reminder of a king who loves the Lord. Judah did not have many good kings, but Hezekiah was one of few who sought to serve the Lord, though imperfectly.

As the Assyrian army surrounded Jerusalem, Sennacherib sent a final message to Hezekiah, telling him not to believe the Lord because He was lying about saving Jerusalem. Sennacherib had been able to defeat the gods of other defeated nations—why would the God of Israel be any different? This is utter blasphemy. Hezekiah's immediate response was to place his trust in the Lord. He tore his clothes, put on sackcloth, and sought Him in prayer at the temple. He praises the Lord of Armies and calls on God to save Judah, so "all the kingdoms of the earth may know that you, Lord, are God—you alone" (Isaiah 37:20). Isaiah tells Hezekiah and his officials that the Lord had promised victory over Sennacherib. The Lord would defend the city for His sake and for the sake of His covenant to David (2 Kings 19:34, Isaiah 37:35). Psalm 76 refers to God's judgment and His mighty defeat of His enemies. The Lord is a fierce and mighty warrior, but He is also personal and close to His people. He makes His dwelling place with them. He is to be feared by the nations.

Not long after the defeat of the Assyrian army, Hezekiah becomes terminally ill. His response, once again, was to turn to the Lord in prayer. Hezekiah begs the Lord to spare his life. The Lord hears Hezekiah's pleas and adds fifteen years to his life. Sadly, Hezekiah did not spend his last years well; he aligned himself with Babylon, the very nation that would carry Judah into captivity. When Isaiah rebuked Hezekiah and told him of the coming judgment of Judah, his only response was that he was glad it would not happen during his lifetime. Hezekiah had become prideful and self-centered. However, whether a good king or a bad king sat on the throne, God's plans would not be thwarted. The true and better King was coming. This King is Jesus, and these chapters teach us to come to Him in prayer and always trust His plan, knowing that He will always do what He has promised.

God's plans would not be thwarted.

WHAT IS YOUR RESPONSE WHEN PEOPLE MOCK THE LORD OR MOCK YOU FOR YOUR FAITH? HOW IS HEZEKIAH'S RESPONSE A GOOD EXAMPLE FOR BELIEVERS TODAY?

HEZEKIAH SOUGHT THE LORD IN PRAYER DURING THE MOST DISTRESSING TIMES OF HIS LIFE. WHEN DO YOU GO TO THE LORD IN PRAYER — DURING GOOD OR BAD TIMES? WHAT HABITS CAN YOU START TO HELP YOU GROW IN YOUR PRAYER LIFE?

DO YOU STRUGGLE WITH APATHY TOWARD OTHERS OR SITUATIONS THAT DO NOT CONCERN YOU? HOW CAN YOU CULTIVATE A HEART THAT DESIRES TO LOVE AND SERVE OTHERS LIKE JESUS?

Isaiah 40-43

THE FIRST THIRTY-NINE CHAPTERS OF ISAIAH HAVE BEEN FILLED WITH WOE AND JUDGMENTS.

However, as we approach Isaiah 40–41, we read of God's forgiveness, power, and tender care for His people. This is a refreshing glimpse of God's character. Our glorious and majestic God has chosen to bestow kindness upon weak, incapable sinners through salvation in Jesus Christ. He does not just forgive us; He puts His love on us. These chapters remind us that because God is loving and just, we do not need to worry or fear. He will not leave us alone. He will walk with us every step of the way and give us everything we need to face this life. Chapters 40–41 also encourage us to remember that the earth and everything in it is passing away, but the Lord and His Word stand forever. His Word became flesh and dwelt among us (John 1:14). His Word, Jesus, brings salvation.

Isaiah 42 contains an introduction to "the servant of the Lord." This is the first of four Servant Songs in Isaiah. This Servant will be a righteous, gentle King, unlike the wicked kings of the earth. Though the original readers would not understand who this coming King was, we know that this gentle Servant King is Jesus. Verse 3 points us to Jesus's immense mercy—He will not break the bruised reed or quench the faintly burning wick. Jesus is a refuge for the weary and a shelter for those bruised by the world. Jesus turns darkness to light and rough places into level ground (Isaiah 42:16). Though God's people rebelled continuously, God would still send a Savior.

In Isaiah 43, the Lord speaks words of love and promise over His people. The first few verses of this passage contain precious promises for Judah and followers of Christ. The Lord promises that He will be with us whenever we pass through overwhelming waters and fires. The Lord also promises Judah that He will work on their behalf and deliver them. Just as He had made a way for Israel's deliverance in the past, God promises to make a way for His chosen people again—He promises to "do something new" (Isaiah 43:19). While the Lord does sustain Judah during their exile and eventually restores them to their home, this "new thing" points to God's plan of salvation in the new covenant of Christ. God would atone for the sins of His people forever through Christ's death on the cross (Isaiah 43:25).

Jesus is a refuge for the weary and a shelter for those bruised by the world.

READ ISAIAH 40:21–24. HOW DO THESE VERSES DISPLAY GOD'S ATTRIBUTES OF SOVEREIGNTY, GLORY, AND OMNIPRESENCE, WHICH MEANS THAT HE IS EVERYWHERE?

HOW DOES THE LIFE OF JESUS SPECIFICALLY FULFILL THE SERVANT SONG IN ISAIAH 42?

READ ISAIAH 43:1–3. HOW DO THESE VERSES ENCOURAGE YOU DURING SEASONS OF HARDSHIP AND SUFFERING?

Isaiah 40–43 67

Isaiah 44–46
Psalm 135

AS WE COME TO TODAY'S READING, WE SEE THAT BLESSINGS CONTINUE TO FLOW FROM THE LORD AS HE PROMISES TO POUR OUT HIS SPIRIT AMONG HIS PEOPLE IN ISAIAH 44.

We have seen this promise before in Isaiah, and it shows us how God will take people who are broken and hardened in sin and give them new hearts (Ezekiel 11:19). The outpouring of God's Spirit will cause His chosen people to "spring up" all around the world (Isaiah 44:4). This is the hope we have received in the gospel. We have received the Spirit of God, and we are called sons and daughters of God.

Isaiah chapters 44–45 remind us that God uses human leaders in His mission of salvation. God declares that Cyrus, the king of Persia, would deliver His people from the hands of Babylon. The Lord makes this promise nearly a century before Cyrus rises to power. Cyrus would be an instrument in the Lord's hand, and the Lord would enable him to have victory over the nations. In the book of Ezra, we will see Cyrus make a decree that a small group, or remnant, of exiles would return to Jerusalem to rebuild the temple. Though God's people were still rebelling during Isaiah's time, He already made a way of deliverance from their future judgment.

Both the last half of Isaiah 45 and Psalm 135 declare God alone is Savior. Israel is called to praise the Lord, for He has chosen them for His possession. God is in complete control of the world and all of its circumstances, and there is no other like Him. He alone is worthy of their adoration, and His name will be known forever. Isaiah 45:23 declares, "Every knee will bow to me, every tongue will swear allegiance." God will vindicate His people and bring salvation.

Though the Lord had loved and cherished His people, their hearts were stubborn and quick to rebel. They fashioned idols, looking to them for the help that only the Lord could provide. The idols and Judah were doomed to the same judgment. They would be carried into a foreign land, and the idols would be unable to save the people. However, though Judah carried their idols, the Lord carried them. The Lord had been with His people since their birth, and He would be with them until they were old and gray. It is the same for us today. The idols of this world will never satisfy us or carry us through the pain and suffering of this life.

> The idols of this world will never satisfy us or carry us through the pain and suffering of this life.

READ ACTS 2:1–4. HOW HAS THE ISAIAH PROPHECY OF THE SPIRIT BEING POURED OUT BEEN FULFILLED FOR ALL BELIEVERS?

HOW DOES GOD'S SOVEREIGN HAND OVER WORLD LEADERS BRING YOU COMFORT AND PEACE DESPITE THE TUMULTUOUS TIMES IN WHICH WE LIVE?

WHAT IDOLS DO YOU CARRY AND REFUSE TO LET GO OF? HOW WOULD RELEASING THEM BRING YOU GREATER JOY AND A CLOSER RELATIONSHIP WITH THE LORD?

Isaiah 44–46, Psalm 135

Isaiah 47–49

IN ISAIAH 47, GOD TELLS BABYLON THAT THEY WILL FALL UNDER HIS HAND INTO JUDGMENT.

While the Lord used Babylon to accomplish His will for the people of Judah, Babylon was prideful, and they put themselves in the place of God. The Lord will also show these people that He alone is God. Babylon is the city that symbolizes the world and all the people who reject God, and their actions and thoughts in this chapter imitate the "prince of this world," Satan. However, the people who reject God and Satan will meet the same end as the original city of Babylon: they will be burned in a consuming fire (Isaiah 47:14, Revelation 20:10). God acts on behalf of His people and brings their enemies to ruin, and God will one day completely wipe away evil from the earth when Christ returns.

The Lord tells His people in Isaiah 48 that He has told them how He will save them so that they will not claim His glorious works as a result of idol worship. He wants them to know that He is the only One who can accomplish salvation for them. The Lord desires their hearts, and though they rebel against Him again and again, He is patient and merciful. Even though they wander, He saves them and gives them the peace and righteousness they could never have on their own (Isaiah 48:18). This is a picture of the gospel of Jesus, where God is glorified by saving sinners and giving them salvation.

Isaiah 49 leads into the second Servant Song, in which we read more promises of Christ's coming. This chapter gives us a glimpse of a conversation between the Lord and the Servant Messiah, who is Jesus. The Lord tells the servant about His mission and what He will accomplish on earth. Though the people of Israel had failed in their role as God's servants, this Servant would be perfect. He would be a light to the nations and would extend salvation to the ends of the earth (Genesis 12:3, Isaiah 2:1–4, Matthew 28:16–20). Jesus would be the restorer of the redeemed people of God. Not only would God bring restoration for the people to their homeland, but through Jesus, we can all experience ultimate restoration to God.

God will one day completely wipe away evil from the earth when Christ returns.

GOD PROMISES HE WILL BRING HIS CHILDREN'S ENEMIES TO RUIN. HOW DOES THIS HELP YOU LEAVE VENGEANCE TO THE LORD? WHAT ANGER TOWARD ENEMIES DO YOU NEED TO RELEASE?

WHEN IS A SEASON YOU HAVE WANDERED FROM THE LORD? HOW DID THE LORD DRAW YOU BACK?

READ LUKE 24:44. HOW DOES JESUS FULFILL ALL THE PROMISES OF ISAIAH 49?

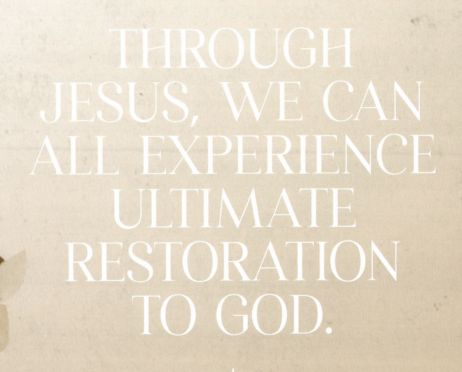

THROUGH JESUS, WE CAN ALL EXPERIENCE ULTIMATE RESTORATION TO GOD.

Isaiah 50–53

IN ISAIAH 50, JESUS CHRIST, THE OBEDIENT SERVANT, RESPONDS TO THE CONVERSATION BETWEEN HIM AND THE LORD IN THE PREVIOUS CHAPTER.

He will perfectly obey what His Father has asked Him to do, despite suffering at the hands of the people He came to save. Jesus knows His Father is with Him. He will seek the Lord's help, and He will accomplish God's purpose. God's chosen people were meant to be obedient servants, but they failed at every turn. Jesus is the greater Israel who will do all the Father asks. He will suffer, die, and extend salvation to the world. The Servant Messiah, Jesus, has allowed us to become servants of the Most High God.

God's salvation of Judah points to the salvation that will come for all of God's people through Jesus Christ. Isaiah 51 shows that the Lord will fulfill His promise to restore Judah to their homeland. And someday, He will bring all people who love Jesus to the eternal city of Zion. The earth and all that is in it is passing away, but the salvation of God will stand forever (Isaiah 51:6).

While Isaiah 52 primarily refers to the return and salvation of the people of Judah from Babylon, its fuller meaning is continued in the final redemption of God's people as they enter the eternal city of Zion. The wicked and unclean, those who have rejected God, will not be able to enter. The family of God will be at peace. God's people will be redeemed by the blood of Jesus Christ.

Isaiah 53 foreshadows the greatest event in history; the suffering servant and His victory over death. This chapter is quoted in the New Testament more than any other passage from the Old Testament. This stunning picture of the Messiah points so clearly to Jesus, who would fulfill every word of this prophecy—a prophecy that was written seven centuries before He was born! Jesus did not suffer because He was guilty but because we were guilty. He is our substitution. He is the One who took what we deserved so that we could be free, and the result of His suffering is our peace and healing. Jesus's sacrifice brings peace to God's people and is an invitation of salvation to the nations. He loves us with an everlasting love, and He has accomplished what we could have never done on our own.

> The Servant Messiah, Jesus, has allowed us to become servants of the Most High God.

IN WHAT WAYS WAS JESUS MORE OBEDIENT THAN GOD'S CHOSEN PEOPLE?
HOW CAN WE BE OBEDIENT SERVANTS TODAY?

READ 1 PETER 1:18–19. HOW DOES THIS REMIND YOU OF ISAIAH 52?
WHY IS SALVATION MORE PRECIOUS THAN ANY GOLD OR SILVER?

SPEND SOME TIME WRITING OUT HOW JESUS FULFILLED THE VERSES IN ISAIAH 53, AND PRAISE HIM FOR YOUR SALVATION AND THE REDEMPTION HE GAVE YOU THROUGH HIS SHED BLOOD. (HINT: YOU CAN REFERENCE MATTHEW 27:27–28:10, MARK 15:16–16:8, LUKE 23:32–24:12, OR JOHN 19.)

Isaiah 54–56

AFTER REVEALING WHAT THE MESSIAH WILL ONE DAY DO FOR THE PEOPLE OF GOD IN ISAIAH 53, THE LORD CALLS HIS PEOPLE TO REJOICE.

As Isaiah 54 explains, the Lord is a faithful husband to His people, and He delights in putting His mercy and compassion on them and showing them everlasting love. The Lord gives His people a picture of what they can look forward to since they belong to Him (Isaiah 54:9–17). Their righteousness will forever be established, and they will experience a covenant of peace with the Lord.

Isaiah 55 opens with a tender call from the Lord for His people to return to Him. And this call is not just for Judah but for "everyone who is thirsty" for the Lord (Isaiah 55:1). The Lord asks the people why they spend their money on things that will never satisfy them when He offers Himself and His everlasting covenant free of charge (Isaiah 55:2–3). The Lord will not only satisfy them, but He will pardon all of the sins of those who desire Him. He will have compassion on those who once rejected Him! Because of what Jesus has done, the call is simple: come. All who are weary, all who are poor, and all who are thirsty are invited to come to Jesus, who can satisfy all of our needs (John 4:10–14).

The Lord's heart for the nations is on full display in Isaiah 56 as God again promises that His salvation and righteousness are coming and will be extended to all people (Isaiah 56:1, 7). The Gentiles who follow Him will be "sons and daughters," and the Lord promises, "I will give each of them an everlasting name that will never be cut off" (Isaiah 56:5). They shall dwell in the house of God forever. This text points to the new covenant that God promises in the Old Testament and fulfills in Christ. In this new covenant, God promises to forgive our sins and restore us to Himself through the death and resurrection of Jesus. Its final fulfillment will be before the throne in heaven with "a vast multitude from every nation, tribe, people, and language, which no one could number, standing before the throne and before the Lamb" (Revelation 7:9).

> Because of what Jesus has done, the call is simple: come.

HOW DOES THE LORD DISPLAY HIS COMPASSION IN ISAIAH 54:10?
WHY CAN YOU TRUST HIS FAITHFULNESS?

HOW DOES JESUS SATISFY YOUR EVERY NEED?

READ MATTHEW 28:19–20 AND ACTS 1:8. HOW ARE BELIEVERS PART OF THE MISSION TO BRING THE NATIONS TO CHRIST? HOW CAN YOU SPECIFICALLY SHARE THE GOSPEL?

Isaiah 57–59

IN ISAIAH 57, THE LORD COMPARES THE LIVES OF THE RIGHTEOUS TO THE LIVES OF THE WICKED.

Though calamity could take away a righteous man, death is not something that worries them because the death of a righteous person sends them to the presence of God (Isaiah 57:2). Belonging to the Lord and walking in righteousness gives a person eternal peace and rest. However, the wicked who pursue the idols of the world have no lasting security because their idols can do nothing on their behalf (Isaiah 57:13). In contrast, the King of kings, our Holy God, offers us Himself as a refuge (Isaiah 57:13, 15). He opens our eyes to see our wickedness and to accept the gospel of peace, but those who remain hardened in their wickedness will know no such peace.

Throughout Israel's history, there were times when the people followed the Lord and times when they did what was right in their own eyes. Isaiah 58 refers to the people doing what was technically right but with hearts that were far from the Lord as they did so. God wanted His people to live and serve Him with pure hearts, but they simply went through the religious motions. Though he lived hundreds of years earlier, King David certainly understood this danger when he prayed, "Search me, God, and know my heart; test me and know my concerns. See if there is any offensive way in me; lead me in the everlasting way" (Psalm 139:23–24). Only when our hearts are made pure will we live for God in the way He desires.

Finally, Isaiah 59 gives us a picture of the hopeless condition of mankind without God. Paul will later remind us of the sin of man and its devastating effects in Romans 3, and he will use Isaiah 59 to support what he says. Isaiah 59 tells us that our iniquities have caused a separation between the Lord and us, and we walk in gloom and are like "the dead" (Isaiah 59:2, 9–10). We do not know the truth (Isaiah 59:15). Since no man was righteous, God intervened. In this hopeless chapter, the gospel is foreshadowed as Isaiah prophesies that God's "own arm brought salvation" (Isaiah 59:16). The person described in verse 17 is clearly Christ as He is the only One who lives righteously and gives His people salvation. Jesus is the Redeemer who destroyed the power of sin, which forever absolved the iniquity that separated us from the Father.

Only when our hearts are made pure will we live for God in the way He desires.

READ PSALM 1. WHAT SIMILARITIES DO YOU SEE BETWEEN PSALM 1 AND ISAIAH 57?

HOW HAVE YOU SIMPLY GONE THROUGH THE MOTIONS OF YOUR FAITH?
JESUS SAYS IN MATTHEW 5:8, "BLESSED ARE THE PURE IN HEART, FOR THEY WILL SEE GOD."
HOW DO PURE HEARTS GRANT US EYES TO SEE GOD?

DO YOU TRULY MOURN YOUR SIN? RECORD SOME OF THE DESCRIPTIONS OF SIN FROM ISAIAH 59:1–16.
HOW DOES JESUS PROVIDE REDEMPTION IN ISAIAH 59:17–21?

Isaiah 60–63

YESTERDAY, WE ENDED BY READING ABOUT CHRIST'S POWER OVER SIN AND THE FREEDOM WE FIND IN THE GOSPEL.

It is the Lord who opens our eyes, softens our hearts, and gives us salvation through His Son. Because of salvation, the earth is no longer our home. We belong to a future heavenly city. The glory of this city and all we have to look forward to is described in Isaiah 60. While this prophecy can first be applied to Judah's return from exile, the text points us—and the people who first heard it—to a future glorious deliverance. The gospel will draw people from every nation, even those who are most hostile to the Lord. There will no longer be violence and suffering. The city of God will be full of peace and righteousness, and the Lord will be our light.

Despite Israel's sin and rejection of the Lord, God promised deliverance through a Messiah. Isaiah 61 announces the good news of the work of the Messiah. The language of Isaiah 61 would have been familiar to the Jews in the context of the year of Jubilee, which was a year of rest that occurred at the end of a seven-year cycle. During the year of Jubilee, prisoners were set free, and debts were forgiven. Jesus is the fulfillment of the year of Jubilee, and He will say this Himself when He goes to teach in the synagogue of His hometown (Luke 4:16–30). In Christ, we are set free, and our debts are forgiven. The Lord takes away our shame, and instead, He clothes us with "a robe of righteousness" (Isaiah 61:10).

In Isaiah 62, the Lord promises His faithful remnant that because He has saved them, He will set them apart in righteousness. God will call His future heavenly kingdom by a new name. And the inhabitants of this kingdom will be like "a glorious crown in the Lord's hand" (Isaiah 62:3). In contrast to this comforting chapter, Isaiah 63 begins with a reminder that the Lord will take vengeance on those who reject Him. Our Savior will one day put to end the evil that has left our world cursed and broken. As we wait, He rains down grace and beckons all people to come and find rest in Him. May these verses stir us to share the good news of Christ with those who do not believe and praise our great God for salvation!

> Our Savior will one day put to end the evil that has left our world cursed and broken.

READ REVELATION 21:22–27. HOW DO YOU SEE ISAIAH 60 FULFILLED IN THESE VERSES?

HOW DOES ISAIAH 62:12 BRING YOU COMFORT, JOY, AND PEACE AS YOU AWAIT CHRIST'S RETURN?

READ REVELATION 19:11–16. HOW DO THESE VERSES FULFILL ISAIAH 63:3–6? IN WHAT WAYS DO THESE VERSES SPARK URGENCY IN YOUR HEART TO SHARE THE GOSPEL WITH OTHERS?

Isaiah 64–66

TOWARD THE END OF ISAIAH 64, A NEW NARRATOR SPEAKS AND ACTS AS AN INTERCESSOR FOR THE PEOPLE.

This intercessor admits that the people have sinned against the Lord, and he asks the Lord not to remember their iniquity forever. Their home was in ruins, and the intercessor asks God to act on their behalf and not be silent toward this destruction. The intercessor's prayer will ultimately be answered in Christ, who will accomplish salvation for God's people through His life, death, and resurrection. Christ alone will allow the iniquity of the redeemed to be forgiven.

In Isaiah 65, the Lord responds to this prayer. God's people have rebelled against Him and walked in their own wickedness. They provoked the Lord and committed gross offenses that displayed their rejection of God. But not all of Judah partook in this rejection of God. There is a faithful remnant of people who will not be destroyed in exile, and the Lord will bring them home. The Lord gives this faithful remnant of Israel a glimpse of the new world that is coming when the presence of sin is finally destroyed. Isaiah 65:17–22 shows us a picture of the millennial kingdom, which is the kingdom of Christ reigning on the earth. While many believers disagree about when this kingdom will take place, the words of this passage cause us to trust that our future in Christ is full of beauty, hope, and restoration.

As the book of Isaiah ends, the Lord reminds His people that His desire is for them to understand who He is and to come to Him in humility and brokenness over their sin. He wants them to fear His Word and obey it. The Lord knows that not all of them will do this, and the judgment foretold in Isaiah for the people of Judah in the southern kingdom would come about. But at the close of the book, we see another vibrant picture of God's everlasting love for His people. While the Lord would bring Judah home from exile, they will eventually dwell in their forever home, New Jerusalem, the city of God. And the Lord will one day bring down a final judgment on the sin of the world, freeing His people from the presence of evil. The meaning of Isaiah's name, "salvation of the Lord," is truly the message of this book. Our God saves!

> Christ alone will allow the iniquity of the redeemed to be forgiven.

HOW DOES GOD'S SALVATION OF THE REMNANT SPEAK TO HIS GRACE?

WHY WAS GOD'S JUDGMENT TOWARD THOSE WHO REJECTED HIM JUST?

REREAD ISAIAH 65:17–22. WHAT ASPECT OF THE NEW CREATION ENCOURAGES YOU THE MOST? HOW DO THESE VERSES GIVE YOU HOPE IN THE PRESENT?

2 Kings 21
2 Chronicles 33

AFTER WRAPPING UP THE BOOK OF ISAIAH, WE TURN OUR ATTENTION BACK TO HEZEKIAH, KING OF JUDAH.

As previously noted, while Hezekiah was not perfect, he is an example of one of the good kings in the history of Israel in Judah. However, the good leadership of Hezekiah was replaced with wicked leadership when his son Manasseh took the throne. Manasseh began to reign at just twelve years old, and he did what was evil in the sight of the Lord. He rebuilt the high places that his father had torn down, placed idols in the temple, and even offered his own sons as burnt offerings. His sin would have dire consequences for the people of God.

The text states that under him, the people of Judah became even more evil than the enemy nations the Lord had destroyed. However, there is a glimmer of hope in Manasseh's story. Despite all of his evil and wickedness, he humbled himself and came to the Lord in repentance. God heard his plea for mercy and received him with open arms. Manasseh's repentance teaches us how, through Christ, God can forgive even the most wicked and wayward hearts. But even though Manasseh repented and removed all of the idols from the city, the people continued to live wickedly.

After Manasseh died, his son Amon took the throne. Like his father, Amon was another evil king who continued to lead the people in wickedness. He made sacrifices to the carved images his father made and served them instead of the Lord. Yet, unlike his father, Amon did not humble himself before the Lord and repent. In doing so, Amon increased his guilt. Soon Amon's wickedness came to an end when his servants rebelled and killed him in his home.

The chapters are upsetting as we continue to see evil kings reign. However, the greatest and most evil kings cannot thwart God's good plans. The plan of God was determined before the world was even formed, and that glorious plan of redemption points us to a better king—a king who would not rule with pride but with humility. This king would not oppress but comfort. This king is Jesus, and our text today makes us long for His kingdom and His reign. Jesus is the only perfect King. He is the only One who can perfectly meet God's holy law and the only One who can lead us in truth and righteousness.

> The greatest and most evil kings cannot thwart God's good plans.

HOW DOES MANASSEH'S REPENTANCE ENCOURAGE YOU TO COME TO GOD IN REPENTANCE?

SECOND CHRONICLES 33:13 TELLS US THAT AFTER GOD FORGAVE AND RESTORED MANASSEH, "MANASSEH CAME TO KNOW THAT THE LORD IS GOD." HOW DOES GOD'S FORGIVENESS REVEAL HIS CHARACTER?

HOW DOES IT ENCOURAGE YOU TO KNOW THAT EVIL LEADERSHIP CANNOT THWART GOD'S PLANS—EVEN DESPITE ANY EVIL LEADERSHIP THAT EXISTS TODAY?

2 Kings 21, 2 Chronicles 33

Nahum 1–3

DURING MANASSEH'S REIGN, GOD ALLOWED MILITARY FORCES FROM ASSYRIA TO CAPTURE AND PUNISH HIM.

But even though God worked through Assyria to lead to Manasseh's repentance, Assyria also needed to repent. In the book of Nahum, God used the prophet Nahum to pronounce the judgment that would come to the evil city of Nineveh in Assyria. God, in His mercy, had given the people a chance to repent generations before when He sent Jonah to them. At that time, they had repented. But they returned to their sin. Now, years later, they threatened God's people, took part in evil rituals, were violent, and ascribed little value to human life. God would judge their wickedness and protect His people.

In the first chapter, Nahum describes the Lord's vengeance against His enemies. This chapter reminds us that God is slow to anger, and He will not pardon the guilty who are unrepentant. He is gracious and merciful, but when the Lord sees evil, He will require justice. Chapter 2 provides details of the collapse of Nineveh. It is a shocking devastation to the city, and its destruction is total and complete.

The book closes with a list of offenses the Lord brings against the people of Nineveh, "the city of blood" (Nahum 3:1). While they have committed atrocities against other nations and even within their own walls, the root of their sin was setting themselves up as higher than any other nation or God (Nahum 3:8–17). The Lord would humble them, and He would deliver the nations from their evil.

Nineveh's fall represents the fall of all people who reject God. Some carry on in rebellion against God, and while it may seem like He does not respond, His ultimate judgment is coming. God is long-suffering, but one day there will no longer be any opportunity to repent. This reality should spur us on to tell others of the good news of Christ. Nahum also reminds us that God is good, and He is a stronghold in times of trouble (Nahum 1:7). We live in a world full of brokenness and evil, and though sometimes we wonder why the Lord allows tragic and horrible things to happen, we can rest in the knowledge that He avenges wrongdoing. We can be confident that our God will do what is right, and He will not let evil go unpunished.

> We can be confident that our God will do what is right, and He will not let evil go unpunished.

HOW DO GOD'S ACTIONS TOWARD ASSYRIA DEMONSTRATE HIS JUSTICE?

WHAT DOES GOD'S LONG-SUFFERING REVEAL ABOUT HIS CHARACTER?

HOW CAN YOU SEE GOD AS YOUR STRONGHOLD IN TIMES OF TROUBLE?

2 Kings 22–23
2 Chronicles 34–35

IN 2 KINGS 22–23 AND 2 CHRONICLES 34–35, WE ARE REMINDED AGAIN THAT THE NATION'S RISE AND FALL WOULD DEPEND ON LEADERSHIP.

These chapters record the triumph of the great king Josiah, who personally experienced the Lord and the power of His Word and then turned the entire nation to the Lord. This young king was one of Judah's best kings, and the text records that he walked in the ways of the Lord just as David did (2 Kings 22:2, 2 Chronicles 34:2).

During Josiah's reign—after he commanded that the temple be repaired—the book of the Law was found after being neglected for some time. The priests went to the prophetess Huldah for instruction, and she shared a message from the Lord. God said He would bring disaster upon His people because of their idolatry, but because of Josiah's humility and obedience, God granted Josiah peace and rescue before the impending disaster.

The words of God were the foundation of Josiah's reign as king, and under Josiah's leadership, the people followed the Lord. During his reign, Josiah restored worship to the Lord, and, like Hezekiah, he tore down the high places and altars of false gods and reinstated the celebration of Passover. Scripture tells us that there was no king like him. His love for the Lord and his leadership of God's people brought revival in the hearts of God's people and impacted the entire culture of Judah at the time. Unfortunately, it seems that the revival was too late, and the kings who followed him quickly returned to doing what was evil in the sight of the Lord.

Josiah was a good king who seemed to bring hope and restoration to the people of Judah. There was no king better than him—at least not an earthly king. But, as the true King of Judah, Jesus would be a true and better king for the people of God. He leads His people with love and grace and is the answer to every covenant promise of God. God would graciously preserve the line of Judah to bring forth the Lion of the Tribe of Judah to rescue and redeem His own. Along the way, He was faithful to be with His people, whether at home or in exile, and we, too, can be confident that our God will not leave us.

> We, too, can be confident that our God will not leave us.

HOW DOES JOSIAH'S HUMILITY ENCOURAGE YOUR OWN HUMILITY?

HOW DOES JOSIAH'S LEADERSHIP DEMONSTRATE THE IMPACT OF FAITHFUL LEADERSHIP UNDER THE LORD?

WHAT QUALITIES IN JOSIAH DO WE SEE IN KING JESUS?

Zephaniah 1-3

THE PROPHET ZEPHANIAH PROPHESIED DURING THE REIGN OF JOSIAH, AND THE BOOK OF ZEPHANIAH FOCUSES ON THE THEME OF THE "DAY OF THE LORD."

In the first chapter, God proclaims His judgment of the land of Judah and the surrounding nations. Judah had rejected the Lord and had sought fulfillment in other gods and pleasures.

As God describes His judgment, it is almost as if He is providing a picture of undoing His own creation (Zephaniah 1:3). Nothing would be able to deliver the people from this terrible day. All of the inhabitants of the earth would come to an end (Zephaniah 1:18). And though we can soberly think of the day that unbelievers will face when Christ returns, we can—if we are followers of Christ—read this chapter in astonishment because we once belonged to the group of people who will one day receive God's wrath. Thankfully, Jesus stood in our place, and He bore our punishment for sin. Judah would face judgment for rejecting the Lord, but that judgment did not come without the promise that one day all would be made right. The Lord's restoration of Judah points to our final restoration through Jesus Christ.

In chapter 2, the Lord provides details of His anger for sin against the nations who do not fear Him. All of the nations that exalted themselves and their gods above the Lord would be humbled. The entire world is under the sovereign hand of God, and there are no nations or people more powerful than He is. While we cannot always see the justice of the Lord at work, He will have the final say, and He will not let injustice go unpunished.

Finally, Zephaniah 3 beautifully shows how God will one day bring all nations to call upon His name and worship in unity. Israel will be restored. Our God will keep His promises. He will gather His people together, and He will rejoice over them (Zephaniah 3:17). We can be confident that this is who our God is. He does not leave us in our sin, but He comes to rescue and redeem us. He brings us hope, forgiveness, and mercy. He brings us Himself. Our God takes broken things and restores them. We can be confident He will do the same for us.

The entire world is under the sovereign hand of God.

HOW DOES ZEPHANIAH 1:1–3 REFLECT THE FLOOD IN GENESIS 6–7?

WHAT SHOULD BE OUR RESPONSE TO THE RESTORATION CHRIST HAS BROUGHT TO OUR LIVES AND THE RESTORATION THAT IS TO COME?

HOW DOES ZEPHANIAH 3:17 GIVE YOU HOPE AS YOU LIVE IN A BROKEN WORLD?

Jeremiah 1-3

JEREMIAH WAS A PROPHET WHO PROPHESIED DURING THE REIGN OF JOSIAH AND HIS SON JEHOIAKIM.

In Jeremiah 1, we see the Lord call Jeremiah to speak His words to the people of Israel. Jeremiah is known as the weeping prophet, but we should remember him as a persevering prophet. In all of the years that he warned Israel of God's coming judgment, there were only two recorded converts.

When Jeremiah first began his ministry, he was a young man given a large and overwhelming task, but the Lord promised to lead him every step of the way. Jeremiah's life would not be easy. He would see Judah's destruction and judgment at the hand of the Babylonians—just as Isaiah had prophesied nearly a hundred years earlier. Then, his countrymen would kidnap him and bring him to the land of Egypt. He would die there and never return home.

The Lord does not waste time in giving Jeremiah a vision. The vision begins with Jeremiah seeing an almond branch. The almond tree was the first to bud in springtime. So, when the Lord shows Jeremiah an almond branch and tells him that He will accomplish His word, Jeremiah knows that God means that His judgment is coming soon (Jeremiah 1:11–12). Jeremiah's next vision of a boiling pot facing away from the north signifies that the judgment will come from the northern people of Babylon (Jeremiah 1:13–14). But, just as Jeremiah receives visions that foreshadow judgment, the Lord also promises Jeremiah's deliverance (Jeremiah 1:18–19).

In chapters 2–3, the Lord reminds Judah of the covenant they have with Him as He describes Judah's faithlessness and idolatry. The people were living in rebellion, but the Lord urged them to return (Jeremiah 3:6–13). They had once delighted in the Lord like a new bride delights in her husband, but they had now forsaken Him (Jeremiah 2:2). They turned their backs on "the fountain of living water" and created their own "cracked cisterns" (Jeremiah 2:13). When Jesus preaches the gospel, He calls Himself the fountain of living water, and He promises that anyone who follows Him would have a well of living water as the overflow of their heart (John 4:13–14, John 7:38). Jesus is our faithful Shepherd King who will bring full and final restoration to God's people (Jeremiah 3:15–18, John 10:11–14).

> Jesus is our faithful Shepherd King who will bring full and final restoration to God's people.

WHAT DOES JEREMIAH'S CALL TEACH US ABOUT TRUSTING IN WHAT GOD CALLS US TO DO, EVEN IF IT IS HARD?

IN WHAT WAYS DO YOU CREATE YOUR OWN "CRACKED CISTERNS"?
HOW CAN YOU TURN TO JESUS, THE FOUNTAIN OF LIVING WATER, INSTEAD?

READ JEREMIAH 3:12. WHAT DOES THIS VERSE TEACH ABOUT GOD'S CHARACTER?

Jeremiah 4-6

AT THE BEGINNING OF JEREMIAH 4, THE LORD SHOWS WHAT WOULD BE THE INCREDIBLE RESULT IF JUDAH WOULD REPENT AND RETURN TO HIM—THE NATIONS WOULD WORSHIP THE LORD AND COME TO KNOW HIM (JEREMIAH 4:1–2).

God chose Israel to stand apart from all the nations so that the whole world would look to their worship of God and be drawn to the Creator. However, they rebelled and rejected the Lord.

Jeremiah anguished over the people's folly. He was known as the weeping prophet because his heart was broken and grieved over the sin and brokenness of God's people. Jeremiah depicts God's judgment by using the same phrase Moses used in Genesis to describe the world before creation: "formless and empty" (Jeremiah 4:23, Genesis 1:2). In a sense, these words foreshadow the Lord's renewal of Judah. The Lord will bring them through a new creation as they return to Him in the midst of their hardship and eventually go back to their homeland. Similarly, Jesus redeems us from the emptiness of our sinful, earthly state and makes us new creations (2 Corinthians 5:17).

Chapters 5–6 of Jeremiah show us the devastating state of Judah and the city of Jerusalem. Though the Lord wants His people to repent and return, there is no righteous person to be found (Jeremiah 5:1, 5). The Lord often compares Israel to a wild vine that does not bear proper fruit, and this should cause us to remember John 15 when Jesus calls Himself the true Vine (Jeremiah 5:10–11, John 15:5). When He comes, Jesus will enable those who believe in Him to have the righteousness they could never possess on their own because He will live perfectly and obey His Father.

Even though the people of Judah—from the young to the old—rejected the Lord, He would promise to not completely destroy them (Jeremiah 5:18). The Lord would preserve a faithful remnant of Israel. Even in His re-emphasis of judgment, He has mercy. This faithful remnant of Israel would contain the line from which the Messiah would eventually come, and this Messiah would deliver us from the fiercest enemies of all: sin and death. Jesus, the Messiah, would be the greater Israel who would remain obedient to God and draw all men and women chosen by God to Himself.

The Lord would preserve a faithful remnant of Israel.

HOW DOES JEREMIAH BEING THE "WEEPING PROPHET" FORESHADOW JESUS? CONSIDER JOHN 11:33–35 AND LUKE 19:41–44.

HOW DOES THE FACT THAT GOD BRINGS ABOUT REDEMPTION FROM EMPTINESS SPEAK TO HIS CHARACTER? WHAT SHOULD OUR RESPONSE BE TO THIS TRUTH?

READ JOHN 15. HOW CAN YOU BEAR FRUIT FOR GOD'S GLORY?

Jeremiah 4–6

Jeremiah 7–9

ONE OF THE REPEATED SENTIMENTS THE LORD DELIVERS TO THE PEOPLE OF JUDAH IS THAT HE HAS OFFERED THEM THE OPPORTUNITY TO REPENT AGAIN AND AGAIN, BUT THEY WOULD NOT.

It is not that they are experiencing this judgment randomly. They have set it up for themselves by their evil deeds and idol worship, which they have also passed down to their children (Jeremiah 7:3, 18). This rebellion is not uncommon and has happened before, even after God delivered Israel from slavery in Egypt (Jeremiah 7:22–24).

In Jeremiah's day, the people of Judah are just like the Israelites, dancing and feasting around the golden calf while Moses met with the Lord on top of the mountain (Exodus 32). They openly disobey God and choose their own gods and pleasure instead of Him. Even worse, the people of Judah are now sacrificing their children to false gods (Jeremiah 7:31). And just as God judged the people of Israel for their idol worship, He will judge the people of Judah.

In Jeremiah 8, the Lord says that the bones of the people killed by the Babylonians will lie before the objects of their worship, which are the sun, the moon, and all of the heavens (Jeremiah 8:1–2). Death is the result of idol worship. The sun, moon, and stars will be able to do nothing for Judah as they are attacked, and the state of their desecrated bodies will be proof. The idols the world turns to today also lead to spiritual death, and they cannot provide any salvation. Only the gospel can save us from ourselves. The gospel calls out our sin and reveals our human condition, and because it does so, we can see our desperate need for Christ and His righteousness.

Jeremiah deeply grieves the state of Judah because God will not spare them. Their fate is sealed. They have forsaken their covenant with the Lord and rejected Him, so now they will answer for their wrongdoing (Jeremiah 9:17–22). They were foolish and relied on themselves when true wisdom is only found in the Lord. We have been faithless as well. We are no better than the people of Judah, but Jesus has borne God's wrath and allowed us to believe and know God. Praise God that He has been merciful to us and saved us from ourselves.

> Praise God that He has been merciful to us and saved us from ourselves.

HOW DO THE MULTIPLE OPPORTUNITIES TO REPENT THAT GOD HAS PROVIDED SPEAK TO HIS GRACE?

WHAT DOES JUDAH'S IDOLATRY—AND OUR OWN IDOLATRY—REVEAL ABOUT SIN?

HOW DOES REMEMBERING THE GOSPEL KEEP US FROM PURSUING DESTRUCTIVE IDOLS?
HOW CAN YOU REMEMBER AND REST IN THE GOSPEL WHEN YOU ARE TEMPTED TO PURSUE IDOLS?

Jeremiah 10–13

THE CURE FOR ISRAEL'S IDOLATRY IS FOR THEM TO GLANCE AT THE BEAUTIFUL CHARACTER OF GOD.

Jeremiah 10 is a stark reminder that there is none like Him. The people had wandered far from God and had clung to idols while also pretending to still worship the Lord. In Jeremiah 11, the Lord tells Jeremiah to speak to the men of Judah and remind them that the promised curse is because they did not honor the covenant, which was their agreement with God. But the men of Judah turned their backs on this truth, and idol worship filled the city that was supposed to be set apart for the Lord (Jeremiah 11:13).

Jeremiah cries out to the Lord in chapter 12 in frustration that the wicked around him seem to be prospering. The Lord tells Jeremiah that things will only worsen, but His judgment against Judah would be severe. However, there is a glimmer of hope at the end of this chapter as the Lord promises that He will again have compassion on Judah, and the nations who destroy them will have to give an answer for laying a hand on the Lord's people.

In chapter 13, the Lord instructs Jeremiah to act out a parable for the people of Judah. He tells Jeremiah to buy linen underwear, which was the noble cloth used by priests, and hide it in a crevice of a rock by the Euphrates River (Jeremiah 13:4). When Jeremiah returned to retrieve the underwear at the Lord's command, it was ruined (Jeremiah 13:7). The Lord tells Jeremiah this is what He will do to Judah's pride. He will bring them low in disgrace. Judah will be forced to cling to the Lord (Jeremiah 13:11).

He also has Jeremiah compare Judah to full bottles of wine. These full wine bottles symbolize the drunkenness of Judah. Instead of being blessed by the Lord, they will be like broken wine bottles dashed against each other (Jeremiah 13:13–14). We are like the broken wine bottle apart from Christ. We are drunk with foolishness and ruined by our sin. We, like Judah, need to be cleansed. And our only true salvation is found by clinging to Jesus.

> We, like Judah, need to be cleansed. And our only true salvation is found by clinging to Jesus.

HOW DOES GAZING AT THE CHARACTER OF GOD HELP US IN OUR STRUGGLE WITH IDOLATRY?

HOW DOES GOD'S COMPASSION THAT YOU RECEIVE IN CHRIST ENCOURAGE YOU WHEN YOU SIN?

READ ISAIAH 64:6, AND REREAD JEREMIAH 13:1–11. HOW DO THESE VERSES MAKE YOU GRATEFUL FOR CHRIST'S GRACE?

Jeremiah 14-17

JEREMIAH 14 SHOWS JUDAH DROPPING INTO DISORDER AS THEY SUFFER FROM DROUGHT AND FAMINE.

The Lord brings these conditions on the people to stir them to repentance. Jeremiah recognizes that the people of Judah have sinned, and he pleads for mercy, but the Lord again tells Jeremiah not to pray for the people. He will not accept their offerings or sacrifices, and they will face judgment.

The days of the prophet Jeremiah were difficult times, and Jeremiah 15 reveals the prophet's discouragement. The very people that Jeremiah wanted to help hated him. Because of their wickedness, they brought judgment on themselves. God did not enjoy the judgment of the people He so deeply loved, but in His justice and holiness, He did what was right. And though Jeremiah did what the Lord had called him to do, the people would not listen.

In Jeremiah 16, God compares Judah's judgment to silencing a wedding feast (Jeremiah 16:9). Throughout Scripture, God describes Himself as a groom and His people as His bride. The silencing of joy at a wedding feast reveals great sadness and heartbreak. The Lord, the faithful groom, has been betrayed by Judah, His bride. What is even more saddening is that the people do not realize that they have betrayed the Lord. They have become worse than their rebellious ancestors, yet the Lord promises restoration (Jeremiah 16:12–15). He will deliver the people of Judah just like He delivered Israel from Egypt.

In chapter 17, Jeremiah draws from the theme of the righteous man described in Psalm 1 to illustrate the sin of Judah. Unlike this righteous man, the people placed their trust in men instead of the Lord; however, kings, armies, and leaders could do nothing for them. We, as humans, are not naturally like the righteous man described in Psalm 1. We commit the same sin that Adam and Eve did in the garden when they desired to have the same knowledge and status as the Lord—yet, all the while, the Lord simply calls us to trust and rest. The righteous man in Psalm 1 and the sin of Judah illustrated in chapter 17 point us toward Jesus, the only person who was perfectly righteous. After we accept Christ as our Savior, the rest of our lives are spent in union and dependency on Him. We can do nothing without Christ, and we become like the people of Judah if we try.

After we accept Christ as our Savior, the rest of our lives are spent in union and dependency on Him.

WHAT DOES JEREMIAH'S OBEDIENCE TO THE LORD—EVEN AMID THE PEOPLE'S UNREPENTANCE—TEACH US ABOUT ENDURANCE IN OUR OWN LIVES?

HOW DOES GOD'S PROMISE OF RESTORATION SPEAK TO HIS FAITHFULNESS?

WHAT DO JEREMIAH 17:5–8 AND PSALM 1 TEACH YOU ABOUT THE BENEFITS OF TRUSTING IN THE LORD? HOW CAN YOU TRUST IN THE LORD OVER MAN?

THE LORD PROMISES RESTORATION.

Jeremiah 18–22

THE LORD SHOWS JEREMIAH THAT HE IS THE POTTER WHO MOLDS HIS PEOPLE IN HIS OWN HANDS IN CHAPTER 18.

In chapter 19, the Lord tells Jeremiah to buy a clay jar from a potter and go to the Ben Hinnom Valley and speak before the elders of the people and priests. The Ben Hinnom Valley was known as a place for worship to the false god Molech. Jeremiah takes the clay jar to this place and smashes it so that it is unmendable. He tells the people that the Lord will do the same to Judah. The Lord previously showed Jeremiah how the people were His clay that He molded, but now, the people are compared to an unmendable clay pot. The people of Judah were unmendable because they hardened their hearts against the Lord, and they allowed horrendous practices of idol worship and child sacrifice to persist.

One of the leading priests, Pashhur, immediately had Jeremiah beaten and humiliated by placing him in the stocks to endure public shame (Chapter 20). This would have signaled to the people that Jeremiah's message was false in the eyes of Judah's highest leaders. Even the priests, the men who represent the people to the Lord, ignored Jeremiah's words and allowed the Lord's name to be smeared by pagan worship. When Pashhur releases Jeremiah, Jeremiah tells Pashhur how all of Judah will fall into the hands of Babylon, and Pashhur and his family will go into captivity.

In chapter 21, Jeremiah speaks to Judah's priests and kings, who are worried over Nebuchadnezzar's advances against them. Jeremiah confirms that Nebuchadnezzar, king of Babylon, is the king who will destroy Judah. Jeremiah also prophesies against the house of David because the kings of Judah had failed. In chapter 22, Jeremiah goes to the king and tells him how God has commanded him to act in justice and righteousness (Jeremiah 22:3). The Lord promised the king that if he were faithful to this command, the throne of David would continue to be filled with kings, but if the king disobeyed, the house would become "a ruin" (Jeremiah 22:5). The kings in the line of David had forsaken the Lord and His covenant with them. Because of this, they would be punished. And while the line of David would experience exile, it would not be destroyed. The Lord would raise a King who would rule with righteousness forever.

The Lord would raise a King who would rule with righteousness forever.

READ I KINGS 9:6–9 AND JEREMIAH 22:8–9. HOW HAVE THE WORDS OF GOD IN I KINGS 9:6–9 COME TO PASS?

HOW DOES GOD BEING OUR POTTER ENCOURAGE US TO SURRENDER TO HIS MOLDING?

WHILE JEREMIAH OBEDIENTLY FOLLOWED WHAT GOD INSTRUCTED HIM TO SAY AND DO, HE OFTEN FACED RIDICULE AND HUMILIATION FROM OTHERS, SUCH AS PASHHUR. HOW CAN YOU CONTINUE TO WALK INTO OBEDIENCE TO GOD, DESPITE THE OPINIONS OR ACTIONS OF OTHERS?

Jeremiah 23–25

IN JEREMIAH 23, JEREMIAH INTRODUCES US TO THE PROMISED KING, WHO IS CALLED THE "RIGHTEOUS BRANCH FOR DAVID" (JEREMIAH 23:5). HE IS THE SHEPHERD KING OF ISRAEL AND JUDAH (JEREMIAH 23:1–5).

This King's name will mean, "The Lord is Our Righteousness" (Jeremiah 23:6). This King's name points to mankind's great need for righteousness, and the only One who could give them righteousness is the Lord. This is a prophecy that speaks directly about Jesus! The redeemed people of God will forever be in the care of Christ—the Righteous Branch and the Shepherd King—who loves and cares for us.

In Jeremiah 24, the exile that Jeremiah has proclaimed comes to fruition. The son of Judah's king, Jeconiah, has been taken into captivity, along with other important officials and tradesmen. The Lord gives Jeremiah another word picture to encourage the faithful remnant from Judah. The Lord shows Jeremiah a basket containing both ripe and rotten figs. The ripe figs are the faithful remnant of people. These figs will go into captivity, but they will return. The Lord will give them new hearts to know and love Him. However, the rotten figs represent those in Judah who have rejected God and will be destroyed.

Jeremiah recounts the ways God's people have rejected him in Jeremiah 25. God had given the people every opportunity to repent and come back to Him, but their hearts were hardened. Now the Lord would send King Nebuchadnezzar of Babylon against them. He even refers to Nebuchadnezzar, a pagan king, as His servant. Judah's surviving people would be in Babylon for seventy years, and then the faithful remnant of Judah would return. God would also turn His judgment on Nebuchadnezzar and all of the nations who had rejected Him.

Jeremiah says they will drink from the cup of God's wrath, which is an image Jesus would later use to describe the cup of wrath He received on the cross (Matthew 26:37–39). What is important for us to understand about Jesus's death is that while crucifixion was a horrible way to die, what made Jesus's death infinitely worse was that He took on the full wrath of God for all the sins of His chosen people. The punishment described in Jeremiah 25 should make us incredibly thankful for Jesus, who took on our punishment in our place. Because of Christ, no believer will ever experience God's wrath—only lasting peace and forgiveness.

> The redeemed people of God will forever be in the care of Christ.

HOW WOULD THE PROMISES OF THE KING IN JEREMIAH 23 BRING HOPE TO JEREMIAH AND THE PEOPLE?

HOW DOES GOD'S USE OF NEBUCHADNEZZAR CONNECT TO HOW HE USED PHARAOH IN EXODUS? WHAT IS SIMILAR, AND WHAT IS DIFFERENT?

WHAT SHOULD OUR RESPONSE BE TO JESUS TAKING THE CUP OF WRATH UPON HIMSELF?

Jeremiah 23–25

Jeremiah 26–29

IN JEREMIAH 26, THE LORD SENDS JEREMIAH TO PROPHESY INSIDE THE TEMPLE COURTS TO ALL THE CITIES OF JUDAH AND EVERYONE WHO CAME TO THE TEMPLE TO WORSHIP THE LORD.

Though the people of Judah carried on with temple festivities, their hearts were far from God. The Lord tells Jeremiah to declare to the people that if they do not listen, the temple will become like Shiloh, and Jerusalem, the city of God, would become a curse. When God says that He will make the temple like Shiloh, He is referring to when the Philistines conquered the city and carried off the ark of the covenant (1 Samuel 4). The priests and temple leaders are angry and want to kill Jeremiah for this message, but when the ruling princes and elders of Judah heard Jeremiah's message, they prevented his execution and told the priests it would be wise to heed Jeremiah's warning.

We read in Jeremiah 27 how God would send Jeremiah to deliver His message that commanded Judah and the surrounding nations to submit to Nebuchadnezzar's rule. Jeremiah would wear an actual yoke before the king of Judah, who, at the time, was conspiring with other nations against Babylon, to remind him that Nebuchadnezzar was who the Lord had chosen to rule over them.

While Jeremiah was a true prophet of God, we learn of a false prophet in Jeremiah 28, Hananiah. Hananiah told Judah that they would only be in exile in Babylon for two years. However, the Lord had already spoken through Jeremiah and said they would be there for seventy. Hananiah was so confident in his message that he took the yoke Jeremiah was still symbolically wearing and smashed it. But just because Hananiah was passionate about his message did not make it true. The Lord would put Hananiah to death that very year because of his false messages.

The people of Judah would go to exile, but Jeremiah would bring a message that they must move forward in the place they found themselves. Babylon would be their new home, and their lives must continue (Jeremiah 29:4–9). Judah's faithful remnant must marry and have children because it will be through their line that the Messiah will come. The Lord had good plans for His people, and He would redeem their brokenness and pain. Their future and hope were secure in Him.

> The Lord had good plans for His people, and He would redeem their brokenness and pain.

HOW DO THE REACTIONS OF THE PRIESTS IN JEREMIAH 26 REVEAL ALL OF HUMANITY'S SINFUL HEARTS?

IN WHAT WAYS DO THE ELDERS CONVINCE THE PRIESTS NOT TO KILL JEREMIAH?

READ MATTHEW 24:23–28. HOW CAN YOU GUARD YOURSELF AGAINST FALSE TEACHERS AND TEACHINGS?

Jeremiah 30–31

YESTERDAY, WE LEARNED HOW EVEN THOUGH JUDAH EXPERIENCED EXILE, GOD HAD PLANS TO REDEEM THEM.

We read in chapter 30 of God's promise for His people's final restoration. Though the promises in this passage point to the future, they would remind God's people—and us—of who He is and what is to come in Jesus. He is our perfect Prophet, Priest, and King. The Lord intended to use this time of exile to discipline Judah for their sin, but He promised that He was always with them to save them (Jeremiah 30:11). God would deliver them, heal them, and bring them peace. Their rescue from Babylon foreshadows the day when Jesus will bring perfect peace to His people once and for all.

The Lord continues to speak of the restoration that He will bring to His faithful remnant in Jeremiah 31. He tells them that He has loved them with an everlasting love and that He has been faithful to them. Throughout this chapter, the Lord continues to give promises of hope and healing to His people. One day, He will bring each of the faithful ones of Judah back to their home after they have been exiled (Jeremiah 31:7–9). This return also points us to when all of the faithful, including those who believe in Christ, will live with God in eternity. The words that the Lord uses to describe how He will care for His people remind us of Christ, our tender Shepherd King, who cares for us by ransoming our lives through the shedding of His blood.

Jeremiah 31:31–40 also tells us of God's new covenant. God promises He will make a new covenant with His people—a covenant unlike the covenants He made with Israel's ancestors. Instead of a covenant written upon stone, God's covenant will be written upon the hearts of His people. Through this covenant, God's people will receive forgiveness and new hearts that would help them walk in faithfulness to the Lord. This new covenant was fulfilled through Christ's death and resurrection. In Christ, we receive forgiveness and new hearts that have God's law written on them. Because of Jesus, we are God's people, and He is our God. And a day is coming when we will dwell with our God forever in a world that will never be uprooted or demolished again (Jeremiah 31:40).

> In Christ, we receive forgiveness and new hearts that have God's law written on them.

WHAT DO WE LEARN ABOUT GOD'S CHARACTER IN THESE CHAPTERS?

WHAT DOES TODAY'S READING REVEAL ABOUT GOD'S DESIRE FOR HIS PEOPLE? HOW HAVE YOU SEEN THIS DESIRE THROUGHOUT YOUR STUDY SO FAR?

HOW DOES JEREMIAH 31:31–40 GIVE YOU HOPE FOR THE PRESENT AND THE FUTURE?

Jeremiah 32–33

IN JEREMIAH CHAPTER 32, THE PROPHET JEREMIAH WAS IMPRISONED BECAUSE ZEDEKIAH, THE KING OF JUDAH AT THAT TIME, WAS FRUSTRATED WITH JEREMIAH'S PROPHECIES OF JUDGMENT.

At the time, Nebuchadnezzar was besieging Jerusalem, and Jeremiah knew that it was only a matter of time before the city came under Babylon's control, just as God promised.

But then, God gave Jeremiah a strange task. He told Jeremiah to buy a field from his cousin in Judah. Jeremiah must have been taken aback by the Lord's request. All of Judah was about to be destroyed; it was hardly the time to make a real estate investment. Jeremiah prayed to the Lord. In his prayer, he praised God, recalling His wonderful works. Jeremiah asked the Lord why he needed to buy the field. And the Lord responded that the Babylonians would be victorious and their armies would ravage Judah. Because of the people's disobedience, the Babylonian army would burn everything, even their idol statues. But after the destruction, after the Lord's judgment, God would bring His people back home.

Jeremiah could buy the field in confidence, knowing that the redeemed people of God would someday return and possess the land. In keeping His covenant promise, the Lord desired to bring His people home and bless them. We can remember this truth as we wander this world before reaching our final home with Christ. The Lord will delight in bringing us home to Him when our time on earth is complete.

The promises of the Lord's restoration continue in chapter 33. The Lord would cleanse His people from their sin, and He would remove evil from His city. Even though the people of Judah were enduring hardship through the exile, this time would ultimately be used for their good. God would purify His people and land. They would no longer be like all the other nations, which were filled with child sacrifice and idol worship. Instead, God would make them a place of joy and glory.

This renewal is what the Lord accomplished through the saving work of Jesus Christ. The Lord promised the survivors of the exile that His Righteous Branch would come (Jeremiah 33:15). The Son of God and Son of David, Jesus Christ, was this Righteous Branch. Through Christ, God restores our hearts from corruption; He brings us who were exiled to sin back home in His presence.

After the destruction, after the Lord's judgment, God would bring His people back home.

REWRITE THE VERSE THAT STICKS OUT TO YOU THE MOST FROM TODAY'S READING.

HOW DOES YOUR SELECTED VERSE HIGHLIGHT THE CHARACTER OF GOD?

HOW DOES YOUR SELECTED VERSE POINT TO FULFILLMENT IN JESUS CHRIST?

Jeremiah 34–38

Editor's Note: The chronology of today's reading may be difficult to follow as it mentions two kings of Judah: King Jehoiakim and King Zedekiah. Both were sons of the good King Josiah. Jehoiakim and Zedekiah ruled at different times, but Scripture makes clear that both were evil kings. By mentioning both of them concurrently, the book of Jeremiah places less emphasis on a linear timeline and more emphasis on the impact of God's prophetic messages to evil kings during this general time period of turmoil.

JEREMIAH 34 OPENS BY DESCRIBING THE LORD'S MERCY TO KING ZEDEKIAH AND JUDAH AS NEBUCHADNEZZAR BESIEGED JERUSALEM.

The Lord told Zedekiah, who ruled after his brother Jehoiakim, that he would die in peace if he obeyed the Lord. But Zedekiah rebelled again by keeping slaves. Zedekiah was not a righteous king, and he did not care for the poor or the oppressed. As a result, Zedekiah deserved an unfortunate fate. The Lord would give Zedekiah over to the slavery he enforced on others.

In chapter 35, Jeremiah contrasts the state of Judah with the faithfulness of the Rechabites. The Rechabites were a radical sect of Israelites who lived in the wilderness and tried to pattern their lives after Israel's early nomads. They lived simple lives in tents and shepherded their flocks. One of their ancestors, Jonadab, commanded them not to drink wine in order to avoid sin. For generations, they obeyed this command. The Rechabites were faithful, and the Lord used their testimony as an example of what He wanted His people to be like. God desired His people's faithful obedience. He wanted them to honor Him as their Father, just as the Rechabites honored their ancestors.

In Jeremiah 36, Jeremiah tells a scribe named Baruch to write down the prophecies from the Lord and read them in the temple. As the people listened, one godly man, Micaiah, heard the words and trembled. Micaiah quickly told the princes of Judah about the prophecies, and they called for Baruch. Baruch read the scroll to them, and they were also greatly troubled. They took the scroll and told Baruch and Jeremiah to hide because they were going to read it to the king, and he would not be pleased. Then, King Jehoiakim comes on the scene. Because of his inclusion in this story, this may be a later retelling of a series of events that happened earlier, as Jehoiakim ruled before his brother Zedekiah. But the main point of this narrative is illustrated in Jehoiakim's response to the words of the scroll; as it was read to him, he burned it, piece by piece.

In chapters 37–38, the timeline shifts again to when Zedekiah first becomes king after his brother's death. The Babylonians started to attack Jerusalem, and Zedekiah pleaded with Jeremiah to intercede to the Lord, but Jeremiah warned Zedekiah that destruction was coming. However, the Lord gave Zedekiah an opportunity to repent.

God did not desire for His people to perish. He wanted to rescue them from their foes, but Zedekiah chose captivity instead. God handed the cruel king over to Babylon. This moment symbolizes our slavery to sin and spiritual evil. But God's plan was not thwarted. God would send a new King, Jesus. Jesus was not a king like Zedekiah. He reigned in righteousness and justice. Under Jesus's Lordship, we who were once slaves are now liberated forever.

HOW DID GOD PROVIDE OPPORTUNITIES FOR THE PEOPLE TO REPENT?

HOW DOES THE STORY OF THE RECHABITES POINT TO JESUS'S OBEDIENCE TO THE FATHER?

WITH THE INDWELLING HOLY SPIRIT, IN WHAT AREAS CAN YOU STRIVE TOWARD OBEDIENCE?

Jeremiah 39–40
2 Kings 24–25
2 Chronicles 36

SECOND KINGS 24–25 AND 2 CHRONICLES 36 SUMMARIZE THE REIGN OF FOUR KINGS: JEHOAHAZ, JEHOIAKIM, JEHOIACHIN, AND ZEDEKIAH. THESE MEN DID WHAT WAS EVIL IN GOD'S SIGHT. AS A RESULT, THE FALL, CAPTIVITY, AND EXILE OF JUDAH WOULD SOON FOLLOW.

The Babylonians finally besieged Judah's capital city of Jerusalem, and though Zedekiah and his family tried to escape, they were chased down and brought before Babylon's King Nebuchadnezzar. The last thing Zedekiah saw was the murder of his children and companions, and then a Babylonian soldier gouged out his eyes and put him in chains. Zedekiah fell to the injustice and slavery that his leadership brought upon others.

As Jerusalem was destroyed, the Babylonians gathered many people and took them into exile. Jeremiah was among the exiles, but Nebuzaradan, the captain of the guard, released him soon after his capture. When Jeremiah arrived in Judah, he saw the fallen kingdom. God's city, which once reflected His glory and beauty, now lay in ruins. The captain of the guard must have known the Lord's prophecies, as he said the destruction was due to the people's sin. The captain offered Jeremiah the chance to live well in Babylon. But Jeremiah remained with the Judeans who were left behind. He chose to stay with those lamenting all that was lost.

Babylon appointed Gedaliah as governor to represent Judah. Gedaliah urged the Judeans not to be afraid. Unfortunately, exiles from other nations were not happy that Babylon kept a remnant in Judah and gave their governor authority. Amidst the destruction, Gedaliah and the remnant had enemies, and thoughts of restoration and progress seemed hopeless.

Nevertheless, these passages end with a reminder of God's grace. The new king of Babylon, Evil-Merodach, pardoned Jehoiachin, who had been deported to Babylon in the first siege. Jehoiachin was elevated in the Babylonian court and dined with the king. Furthermore, after the Persian empire replaced Babylon as the leading empire, King Cyrus of Persia made a decree that the temple in Jerusalem could be rebuilt.

Even when all hope seemed lost, the Lord was there, keeping His covenant with His people. This God is our God. He is a God of restoration and redemption. The promise of a New Jerusalem temple was fulfilled in Jesus Christ, who is the King for whom our hearts long. Jesus is the One who returns us to God. His body is what the Jerusalem temple symbolized. In Jesus, we find hope and rest from the threat of evil.

HOW DOES ZEDEKIAH'S SIN HIGHLIGHT THE SIN OF MANKIND?

WHAT WERE GOD'S PURPOSES FOR THE BABYLONIAN CAPTIVITY?
HOW DID THIS TIME OF EXILE AND CAPTIVITY DEMONSTRATE GOD'S GOOD CHARACTER AND PLAN?

HOW DO THESE PASSAGES ENCOURAGE YOU WHEN HOPE SEEMS LOST?

Psalms 74, 79

PSALMS 74 AND 79 HIGHLIGHT THE LAMENT THAT OCCURRED DURING THE BABYLONIAN INVASION.

Though chaos pervaded the land, people were moved to voice their emotions through poetry and song. In their worship, the psalmists kept their focus on God's character and promises. They fought for hope when it seemed nowhere to be found.

Both Psalm 74 and 79 are attributed to a man named Asaph. As mentioned in *Eden to Eternity: Volume 2*, Asaph was a Levite appointed by David to be a worship leader in the tabernacle. With this insight, as we continue to move through Scripture chronologically, it might seem odd to read a psalm of Asaph amid events that happened centuries after he lived. However, some scholars believe "Asaph" might also be used as a general title, passed down through the generations, to refer to the temple singers who came after him and continued his legacy of penning songs on behalf of the Israelites. Though this context is helpful for us to understand, for the sake of clarity, we will continue to refer to the author of this psalm simply as "Asaph."

Psalm 74 reflects on the destruction of the temple of Jerusalem. The temple represented God's presence with the people of Israel. Under King Solomon's reign, the people built the temple with God's intricate plans. The temple was ornate, mirroring the glory of God and His heavenly kingdom. But after the siege, Jerusalem was burned to the ground and now a pile of rubble. The loss was devastating for the people of God. At first, in his agony, Asaph questioned the Lord and pleaded with Him to destroy their enemies. He wondered for how long God would allow His people to be mocked.

However, Asaph also recounted God's faithfulness and His power. He asked the Lord to remember His covenant promise. Scripture states, "Consider the covenant, for the dark places of the land are full of violence. Do not let the oppressed turn away in shame; let the poor and needy praise your name" (Psalm 74:20–21). God did not find pleasure in the Babylonian oppression against His people. However, He most of all was not pleased by their sin, and the Babylonian invasion served as judgment. In His time, God would not only free His people from Babylon, but He would also free His people from sin. He kept this covenant in Jesus Christ. Jesus is the embodiment of the Jerusalem temple, as He is God in the flesh, dwelling with His people. His saving work saved us from sin and brought us back to God's presence.

Psalm 79 is considered a companion psalm to Psalm 74. The psalm gives detailed descriptions of the destruction of the holy city, but it also laments the sins of the people who caused the destruction to occur. Asaph and the people cry out, "How long, Lord?" (Psalm 79:5). We, too, cry out these words, though we read this psalm knowing that God has delivered His people from sin through Jesus. We still see evil and the presence of sin in the world, and we groan with creation as we wait with the people of God for our King to return.

CHOOSE A VERSE FROM THESE PASSAGES, AND PARAPHRASE IT IN YOUR OWN WORDS.

HOW DOES THE GOSPEL SPEAK TO THE MAIN POINT OF THE VERSE YOU PUT INTO YOUR OWN WORDS?

HOW DOES WORSHIP HELP YOU THROUGH LAMENT?

Habakkuk 1–3

IN ADDITION TO THE POETS, PROPHETS ALSO CRIED OUT TO THE LORD IN PRAYER DURING THE EXILIC PERIOD.

The prophet Habakkuk expressed this lament through his prophetic message from the Lord. Habakkuk lived in the southern kingdom of Judah and saw God's people become like other wicked nations. In the first chapter of the book, Habakkuk cried out to the Lord about injustice being unanswered.

He saw that God's chosen people were rebelling against Him and hurting those who were faithful to God, and he wondered why the Lord seemed to do nothing about it. Habakkuk was open and honest with the Lord, and the Lord was quick to respond to him. The Lord told the prophet that because of Judah's sin, they would be enslaved by the Babylonians, also known as the Chaldeans (Habakkuk 1:6).

Habakkuk then questioned the Lord. As you read his words, you can see that he was overwhelmed by the fact that the Lord was using the evil Babylonians to judge His people. Habakkuk's doubts and fears were on full display.

Habakkuk's lament for the nation is so helpful for us to read. Habakkuk lived the reality of every human being in a broken world. We, too, are often overwhelmed with the effects of evil all around us, but we know that we are secure in Christ.

Habakkuk 2:4 is one of the most well-known phrases in Scripture: the righteous shall live by faith. The verse is quoted three times in the New Testament (Romans 1:17, Galatians 3:11, Hebrews 10:38). In Habakkuk 2, the Lord reminded the prophet that even though he could not see everything the Lord was doing, he could trust Him; while evil might have seemed to be undefeated, it would never win. Babylon would have to answer to the Lord for their sin. The Lord promised a day when instead of the earth being filled with evil, it would be filled with His glory.

Habakkuk ended with a prayer, showing his confidence in the Lord. The last verses of the book encourage us that we can praise the Lord no matter what we face. We may not understand God's plan, but our eternal security and peace are in God. When Jesus returns, He will bring God's judgment upon the earth, but He will also fill it with the glory of God (Habakkuk 2:14).

We know that we are secure in Christ.

HOW ARE HABAKKUK'S WORDS SIMILAR TO ASAPH'S IN PSALM 74?

IN WHAT WAYS DOES READING ABOUT THE EXILE FROM THE PERSPECTIVE OF THE POETS AND PROPHETS BRING TO LIGHT THE NATURE OF HUMAN SIN AND OUR REACTION TO ITS CONSEQUENCES?

WHAT VERSE STICKS OUT TO YOU THE MOST FROM CHAPTER 3? WHAT INSIGHT DOES THIS VERSE REVEAL ABOUT GOD'S CHARACTER?

Jeremiah 41-45

THE BABYLONIANS APPOINTED GEDALIAH TO GOVERN JUDAH, BUT JEALOUSY AND BITTERNESS FROM NEIGHBORING ETHNICITIES LEAD TO HIS MURDER.

Gedaliah's murder happened at the hand of Ishmael (Jeremiah 41:1–3). Ishmael also killed and plumaged innocent people after Gedaliah's death. These events highlight a descent into chaos as a result of Judah's disobedience.

The chaos of Gedaliah's death and Ishmael's insurrection was yet another reminder that the people needed God's Messiah. A man named Johanan rescued the people of Judah from Ishmael (Jeremiah 41:11–18), but he was not the Messiah. Afterward, Johanan and his army approached Jeremiah and asked for guidance. The men told Jeremiah they would obey whatever the Lord said. The Lord was clear that the people were to stay in the land and that He would protect them. But the people rejected his counsel. Johanan and his army led the people away to Egypt. Egypt was a place that indicated the people's turn away from the Lord instead of their trust in Him. This place also symbolized the people's slavery to sin. There, the Israelites would be tempted to worship other gods. They chose to follow the darkness that comes from being away from God.

The Lord prophesied that He would send the Babylonians to take over Egypt as just punishment for Egypt's and Israel's sins. In Jeremiah 44, the prophet spoke directly to Judah about their idolatrous behavior against the Lord. The people who went to Egypt to seek refuge and continued in idol worship would face destruction. However, not all of Judah would be destroyed, and there would be yet another remnant of Judah who would escape.

In Jeremiah 45, the Lord told Baruch, Jeremiah's scribe, that even though destruction surrounded him, God would deliver Baruch. We can assume Baruch had faith in the Lord during this time. God's message to Baruch shows the Lord's commitment despite the people's continued sin. Jesus gives a similar message to us who follow Him. We do not need to run to the world for comfort and protection. Instead, we must run to our God, who is the One who will guide and protect us right where He has called us to be. The Lord will never stop being faithful to us. We are challenged to set our minds on heaven and the glory of God instead of ourselves. We can trust in Him as our strong refuge.

The Lord will never stop being faithful to us.

WHAT DOES THE PEOPLE'S RETURN TO IDOLATRY REVEAL ABOUT HUMAN NATURE?

WHEN ARE TIMES IN WHICH YOU ARE TEMPTED TO REJECT GODLY COUNSEL AND RELY ON YOURSELF?

HOW CAN YOU LEAN ON JESUS CHRIST IN THOSE MOMENTS?

Jeremiah 46-48

TODAY, WE BEGIN TO READ A SERIES OF JUDGMENTS THE LORD PRONOUNCED TO NATIONS OUTSIDE OF JUDAH.

God heard the prayers of His people, like Asaph and Habakkuk, and He would punish these nations for their oppression toward His people.

Today's chapters address judgment for Egypt, Philistia, and Moab. As we have seen in redemptive history so far, these nations were considered enemies of Israel. They were wicked and idolatrous nations. In other words, they were not only unjust, but they also did not worship the one true God. The language used here captures utter destruction against evil.

The Lord pronounced judgment on Egypt first. He had just spoken to His people about the destruction that was coming there. At the end of the judgment, the Lord gave His faithful remnant of people hope. Though they fled to the land that had once held their ancestors captive, the Lord would deliver them again. They would face discipline for their sin against Him, but He would not completely destroy them. God promised that His chosen people's fate would be unlike the other nations surrounding them. Their ancient enemies, the Philistines, and their wandering cousins and neighbors, the Moabites, would be completely overcome by Babylon. Even though some of the Moabites would be allowed to return from captivity, the nation would never return to what it once was.

The Lord did not delight in pouring out this judgment on the nations, but He is just. The sin these nations committed was grievous, and they displayed no desire to repent. We must remember that the nation of Israel had been among the Philistines and Moabites for generations. God had given these foreign nations the opportunity to repent and turn to Him as they observed His chosen people, but they refused.

The judgments served as a shadow of the coming judgment that will happen when Jesus returns to earth to destroy evil once and for all (Revelation 20:11–15). The Lord repeated patterns throughout biblical history so that people would recognize the truth, repent, and turn to Him. Witnessing Judah's destruction, the nations could see the Lord was the one true God. As we read these chapters, it is important to remember that no human being, besides Jesus, is innocent. We all are sinful, and we are all deserving of God's wrath. The judgment written in these chapters is the judgment we deserve, and yet, Jesus stood in our place. He took our sin so that we could be covered in His righteousness.

> Jesus stood in our place. He took our sin so that we could be covered in His righteousness.

HOW DOES GOD'S RESPONSE TO EVIL PROVIDE YOU COMFORT?

HOW DO YOU RESPOND TO THE GOSPEL COVERING YOU FROM THE LORD'S RIGHTEOUS JUDGMENT?

HOW DID THE PRIDE OF EGYPT, PHILISTIA, AND MOAB ULTIMATELY LEAD TO THEIR RUIN?

Jeremiah 49–50

THIS SECTION OF SCRIPTURE CONTAINS JUDGMENTS AGAINST MORE NATIONS: AMMON, EDOM, DAMASCUS, KEDAR, HAZOR, AND BABYLON.

Through Jeremiah, God spoke of punishment toward Ammon. The Ammonites were among the people who were hostile toward Gedaliah. This group was an old enemy of the people of Israel. But after their punishment, God promised to restore their fortunes. Next was Edom. The Edomites were the descendants of Jacob's estranged brother, Esau. The Edomites assisted Babylon in destroying Judah. Throughout the Bible, the Edomites represented those who rejected belief in God. At the end of God's prophecy, there was no restoration for the Edomites. Similarly, without faith, it is impossible to experience the blessings of God's presence. Edom would instead meet complete desolation. The next judgments were for the cities within the Syrian and Arabic kingdoms. These nations would fall to Assyria and Babylon.

The harshest of all the judgments went to Babylon. Babylon was infamous for its power, and yet, God ordained it to carry out His judgment decree on the nations. But Babylon was not more powerful than the sovereign Lord. Babylon would face punishment for coming up against God's people and burning down His temple. The Lord would go to war against the Babylonian kingdom, as Babylon promoted the kingdom of darkness. The Babylonians would be humbled before the Lord. Cyrus, the king of Persia, was God's chosen instrument to fulfill the Lord's decree on Babylon.

God's judgment of the Babylonians is significant because they represented spiritual evil. The Babylonians were agents of Satan who wanted God's creation to turn from His goodness. The Lord's judgment foreshadows the final judgment Jesus will bring when He returns to earth. Then, the destruction of Babylon will be sudden and swift, ending the reign of evil's tyranny and forever silencing the serpent. The language around the destruction of Babylon points to the New Testament's language describing the last days, which will come like "a thief in the night" (1 Thessalonians 5:2). Only the Lord knows the time and day Jesus will return.

> Babylon was not more powerful than the sovereign Lord.

WHAT ATTRIBUTE OF GOD'S CHARACTER IS SHOWN THROUGH AMMON'S RESTORATION (JEREMIAH 49:6)?

THE KINGDOM OF DARKNESS IS BEHIND THE CHAOS AND CONFLICT OF OUR AGE (EPHESIANS 6:12). HOW DOES THIS TRUTH IMPACT YOUR PRAYER LIFE?

HOW CAN YOU LIVE WITH THE HOPE OF JESUS'S SECOND COMING?

Jeremiah 51–52

IN THE LAST TWO CHAPTERS OF JEREMIAH, WE ARE SHOWN THE FUTURE OF ISRAEL, JUDAH, AND BABYLON.

The Lord tells us Babylon, a mighty nation of great conquerors, is nothing compared to Him. He used Babylon to punish His people, but then He will punish Babylon for her sins, as well. Babylon seemed like an unstoppable dynasty, but the Lord was above Babylon. Babylon was simply a tool in His hand, and it would be held accountable for its sins.

In our lives, we see and experience evil. We may wonder if God is sovereign over the atrocities we observe. He is. He uses all things to accomplish His plans and purposes, even evil. And we know that one day He will do away with all evil once and for all. The prevalent evil of this world may seem like it will win, but we know that Jesus is victorious. He will defeat all evil forever, and He will lead His people back to Zion, the eternal city of God (Romans 11:26).

After the Lord pronounces His judgment on Babylon and His faithfulness to His people in chapter 51, we see even more details than we did before of the fall of Jerusalem to Babylon in chapter 52. This was a grisly sight filled with savage war, famine, imprisonment, and death. And that is only the first eleven verses. The chapter then goes on to recount the destruction and plundering of the temple and the exile of the people to Babylon.

Nebuchadnezzar may have burned the grand and glorious temple Solomon built for the Lord, and even though God's people would rebuild a second temple, a temple would soon no longer be necessary. Jesus gives us access to the Lord, and He dwells in our hearts through the Holy Spirit. Jeremiah shows us God's judgment for His people, but it is not without hope!

Jeremiah 52 does not end in destruction. The last section of this chapter is all about hope. Judah's King Jehoiachin is pardoned by the king of Babylon. This is a recounting of the same event we learned about when we previously studied Jeremiah 39–40, 2 Kings 24–25, and 2 Chronicles 36. Jehoiachin is brought out of his prison cell, changed from his prison clothes, and given a seat at the king's table. He was given a portion or allowance every day. Yet this is only a small foreshadowing of the grace that God would one day bestow on His people through Jesus Christ. One day, Jesus would come to be the true freedom God promised to His people.

> Babylon seemed like an unstoppable dynasty, but the Lord was above Babylon.

WHAT DO YOU THINK THE PEOPLE OF GOD FELT WHEN JERUSALEM FELL TO BABYLON?
IS THERE A TIME IN YOUR LIFE WHEN YOU FELT SIMILAR EMOTIONS?

WHY DO YOU THINK GOD PRONOUNCED JUDGMENT ON BABYLON?
WHAT DOES THIS TELL YOU ABOUT GOD?

READ I CORINTHIANS 6:19. WHERE IS GOD'S TEMPLE TODAY?

Lamentations 1-3

LAMENTATIONS IS A BOOK OF POETRY WRITTEN AFTER THE FALL OF JERUSALEM.

There are five poems in acrostic form, which means that certain letters in each line form a word. In this case, each verse begins with a letter of the Hebrew alphabet in successive order. This pattern is broken in the fifth poem. However, there are still 22 verses, with each verse representing a letter of the Hebrew alphabet. This shows us that the author of Lamentations is covering the topic of suffering as much as he can.

Though the author of Lamentations is unknown, many commentators attribute it as being written by Jeremiah. The author grieved over Judah's rejection of the Lord, and he wept over the destruction of the cherished city of Jerusalem. God's people had too many "lovers" instead of clinging to their true love, the Lord. They rejected their covenant with their faithful God for unfaithful companions who would leave them.

As a result, the city of Jerusalem was destroyed because of their sins. The first poem describes Jerusalem as a woman who sits in shame and nakedness. The state of Jerusalem reminds us of the natural consequences of sin and rebellion against God. It also foreshadows the grief and suffering that Jesus will bear for us on the cross as He takes on the sins of the people of God. He, too, will face rejection from the Lord, but because He conquered sin, He can bring all the people of God back to their eternal home in Zion. The city that the author describes will not be sad forever. It will be restored at the end of days in Christ.

Chapter 2 provides detail after detail about how the Lord has come against Judah, and this in itself causes us to cry out to Jesus in thanksgiving for what He has done on our behalf. The wrath described in this chapter is what we deserved, but Jesus stood in our place. Yet we still need to mourn over our sin and the havoc it causes. Before we are saved, our sin causes a separation between God and us. But God does the unthinkable through the gospel. While He could war against us, He acts as our Redeemer and saves us from ourselves. Our God is gracious above measure.

Chapter 3 of Lamentations is the center of the book, and it is the focal point of the author's message. The author spends the first two poems deeply lamenting Judah's sins, and in the third poem, he actually begins by taking on the weight of Judah's sin. His language foreshadows Christ as the suffering servant on our behalf. After this, the author does what we must do as well. He remembers who God is, and He finds hope in God alone. He found confidence and hope in the unchanging character of our God, who never changes, for His mercies are new every day, and His faithfulness never fails (Lamentations 3:22–23). We must do the same. While grief over sin is a healthy practice in the believer's life, we are covered in the faithfulness and mercy of God. This is the hope that allows us to press on. God redeems us!

God does the unthinkable through the gospel.

ARE YOU COMFORTABLE WITH EXPRESSING YOUR GRIEF TO THE LORD? WHY OR WHY NOT?

READ LAMENTATIONS 3:19–24. WRITE DOWN A LIST OF WORDS THE AUTHOR USES TO DESCRIBE HIS GRIEF. THEN WRITE DOWN A LIST OF THE WORDS USED TO DESCRIBE THE FAITHFULNESS OF GOD. WHAT DOES THIS TELL YOU ABOUT HOW GOD CARES FOR THOSE WHO GRIEVE?

WRITE A PRAYER TO THE LORD EXPRESSING ANY GRIEF YOU ARE CURRENTLY EXPERIENCING. ASK GOD TO REVEAL HIS FAITHFULNESS TO YOU, EVEN IN THE MIDST OF GRIEF.

Lamentations 1–3

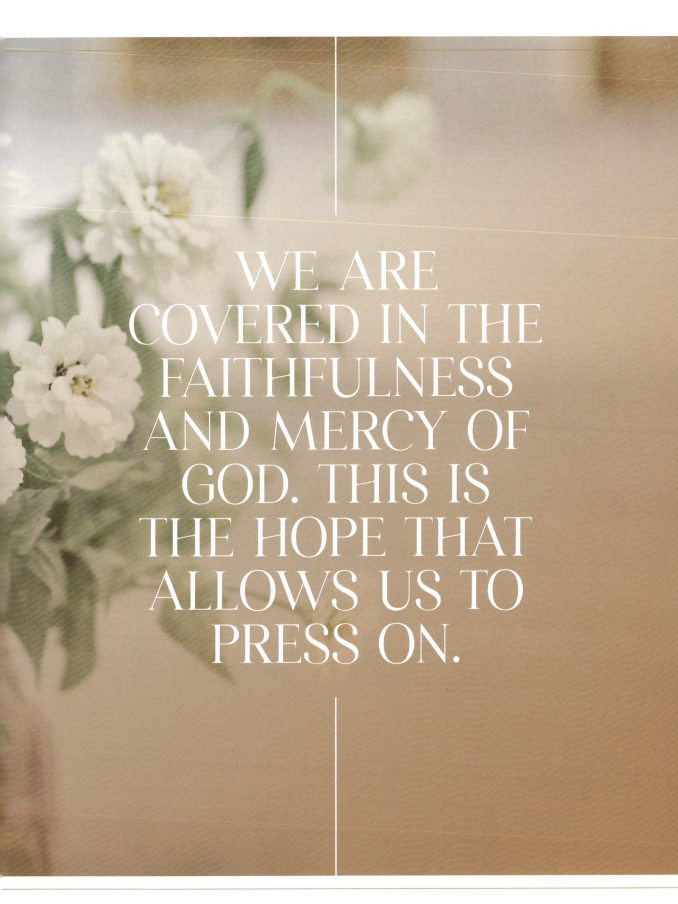

WE ARE COVERED IN THE FAITHFULNESS AND MERCY OF GOD. THIS IS THE HOPE THAT ALLOWS US TO PRESS ON.

Lamentations 4–5

THE LAMENTATION IN CHAPTER 4 REMINDS US HOW THE PEOPLE OF JUDAH HAD GIVEN UP EVERYTHING TO GO THEIR OWN WAY.

For generations, the Lord loved and protected His chosen people. He called them in the time of Abraham, delivered them from the bondage of Egypt, and brought them into the Promised Land. He had been with them every step of the way, and yet they turned away from His love. He had never broken His promise, yet they tossed it aside. The world looked at Israel and saw them as untouchable because the Lord was on their side. Israel believed this as well, but they were not untouchable to the Lord. He was the only One who would allow true and lasting destruction to fall on them by His hand.

The effect of this destruction is detailed throughout the fourth poem, and it is heartbreaking. The nation of Judah had fallen into chaos and disorder. Yet God gives hope to His people by telling them that their destruction has been "accomplished." It would not go on forever. This foreshadows the accomplishment of Christ on the cross. When Jesus says that it is finished as He takes His last breath and then resurrects from the dead three days later, the world sighs in relief. The curse of sin has been conquered, and while we still feel its presence from day to day, it does not control us anymore. We are made into new creations in Christ.

Chapter 5 contains a prayer from Jeremiah as he pleads with the Lord to remember His own. Though chastening was necessary, the Lord will never once forget His own. The situation was bleak, but the author and the remnant of God's people could see His glory shine through, even in captivity. It would be seventy years until the captivity ended, and yet even in captivity, the Lord was faithful.

This fifth and final poem reminds us of the state of the world. Each day, we see how sin has taken its toll on the world around us, and we wonder when it will end. Like the author, we can cry out, "Restore us to yourself, O Lord" (Lamentations 5:21, ESV), and we can know that He will! When we are in Christ, sin no longer separates us from the Lord, even though we experience sanctification until the day we die. One day, when Christ returns to earth, the Lord will restore all things, and we will be with Him forever. Lamenting over sin will cease, and there will only be rejoicing over the Lord's graciousness and mercy.

The Lord will never once forget His own.

ACCORDING TO LAMENTATIONS 4, THE PEOPLE DID NOT BELIEVE GOD WOULD PUNISH THEM FOR THEIR SINS, BUT THEY FOUND OUT THE HARD WAY THEY SHOULD HAVE BELIEVED GOD AND REPENTED. TAKE A MOMENT TO SEARCH YOUR HEART. ARE THERE ANY SINS YOU HAVE NOT YET REPENTED OF BEFORE THE LORD?

WHAT WORDS OR PHRASES THAT EXPRESS GRIEF IN LAMENTATIONS 4–5 COULD YOU RELATE TO? LIST EACH ONE AND WHY YOU RELATED TO IT.

WITHOUT CHRIST, WE WOULD ALL RECEIVE THE SAME JUST PUNISHMENT FOR OUR SINS THAT GOD'S PEOPLE LAMENTED IN LAMENTATIONS. WRITE A PRAYER THANKING GOD FOR THE SALVATION OFFERED IN JESUS.

Ezekiel 1–4

THE BOOK OF EZEKIEL BEGINS WITH THE WORD OF THE LORD COMING TO EZEKIEL WHEN HE WAS AMONG THE EXILED PEOPLE IN BABYLON.

Already, this is a beautiful reminder that the Lord has not forgotten His people in Babylon. As Ezekiel sits by a canal, he sees a stormy wind approach him, and then clouds and fire appear all around it. It opens, and through the center, the attendants of the Lord—the cherubim—begin to appear.

As the vision continues, he begins to see divine wheels full of eyes moving all about. Ezekiel is seeing the divine chariot of the Lord. This symbolizes how God is going to war. Then Ezekiel sees the throne of God, and he sees One taking the form of a man sitting upon it. Ezekiel is seeing the Savior of the world, who is yet to humble Himself from His heavenly position and take on flesh. Jesus truly is seen throughout the Old Testament!

As Ezekiel stands stunned by what He sees, the Lord calls out to him and tells him that He has called him to speak. The Lord puts His Spirit inside of Ezekiel, just as He will one day put His Spirit inside of all those who believe in Him. The preincarnate Christ, the Word of God, gives Ezekiel His own Words in the form of a scroll to bring to the people of Israel. And sadly, just as people reject Christ's words in the New Testament, they reject the messages that Ezekiel brings.

In chapter 3, the Lord commands Ezekiel to eat the scroll, and he does. The scroll is as sweet to him as honey. This represents how the Word of God is our daily food. It sustains us and helps us grow. But it is both sweet and bitter. It is sweet with encouragement and life-giving truth, and it is bitter with conviction and instruction. We soon discover that Israel wanted only the feel-good words from false prophets instead of the life-giving words of God.

The hearts of the people of Judah were hardened to the truth, so in chapter 4, Ezekiel uses action sermons instead of words. He acted out his messages to the people and showed them the calamity they faced from God's hand. One of the first actions the Lord commands Ezekiel to do is to create a miniature model of the city with tiny platforms around it, representing the siege of Jerusalem the Lord had promised. Ezekiel would then lay bound on his side, facing away from the city, with a cooking grate between him and the tiny model. With this demonstration, Ezekiel represents the Lord's decision to bring judgment upon His people. The scenes in Ezekiel are not the only time we will see God turn away from His people. In Matthew 27:46, we will see God turn away from Jesus as Jesus bears our sin on the cross. Jesus took our filth and shamefulness and covered us with His righteousness.

> Jesus truly is seen throughout the Old Testament.

GOD COMMANDED EZEKIEL TO "EAT THE SCROLL" OF THE WORD OF GOD AND THEN "GO" AND "SPEAK." READ MATTHEW 28:19–20. WHAT SIMILARITIES DO YOU SEE BETWEEN EZEKIEL'S COMMISSION AND THE GREAT COMMISSION IN MATTHEW 28?

READ EZEKIEL 3:26. WHY DO YOU THINK GOD INSTRUCTED EZEKIEL TO PROCLAIM HIS MESSAGE THROUGH "ACTION SERMONS"? HOW DO YOU IMAGINE PEOPLE REACTED TO THESE MESSAGES?

THE PHRASE "THE WORD OF THE LORD CAME TO ME" APPEARS ALMOST FIFTY TIMES IN EZEKIEL. HOW DO YOU THINK THE WORD OF THE LORD COMES TO US TODAY?

Ezekiel 5–8

Editor's Note: In yesterday's reading, we learned that the prophet Ezekiel is already in captivity in Babylon, but in today's reading, we see Ezekiel prophesy about the people of Judah being captured and exiled by the Babylonians. At first glance, these events may seem to be out-of-order. However, while Israel and some of Judah had already been captured and exiled, the capital city of Jerusalem did not fall until about a decade later. With this in mind, we can understand that Ezekiel was likely prophesying about the final collapse of Jerusalem.

IN EZEKIEL, WE SEE MESSAGES SURROUNDING GOD'S JUDGMENT AND MERCY.

Ezekiel shows this in chapter 5 when he shaves his head to symbolize what the nation was facing. A third of his hair he burned because a third of Jerusalem would die as the city burned to the ground. A third of his hair he cut with a sword because a third of the people would die at the Babylonians' hands. The remaining third of his hair was scattered in the wind. But from this third, he took a small bit of hair and carefully tucked it into the hem of his garment as a reminder that God would save some of the people and allow them to one day return to their homeland. God's faithful remnant of people would be spared, just as He promised, and eventually, He would bring the Messiah out of Judah.

In Ezekiel 6, the Lord promises that Israel's spiritual death caused by idol worship will become a physical reality. The bones of those who had worshiped idols in Judah would be laid before the idols' altars after the destruction of the city. The land would be purged of evil by the sword, disease, and famine, and those who had rejected the Lord and worshiped false gods would know that the Lord alone was worthy of worship.

In Ezekiel 7, the Lord declares that the day for judgment has come. There was no more time for repentance. The people had been given every opportunity to repent and turn to Him, but they refused. The judgment for their sin would be great at the hands of the Babylonians. This judgment points us forward yet again to the judgment that will come at the end of days when Christ returns. There will be a time where there is no more opportunity to repent (Luke 14:15–23). While believers do not need to fear this time because we are secure in the righteousness of Christ, this should make us fearful for those who do not know Christ and have rebelled against Him. This finality is a serious matter, and we should think of it often as we interact with unbelievers. Judgment is coming, and there are lost souls who need to hear the good news that has changed our hearts and lives.

The people of Judah thought that their idolatry was hidden, but the Lord reveals to Ezekiel in chapter 7 that the leading elders are sacrificing to false gods in the Lord's temple. They either believed that the Lord did not care that they did so or that He did not see it happening, which is why they continued to do this in secret. Every action we take, every thought we think, and every word we say are on display before the Lord.

Chapter 8 begins Ezekiel's second vision, which has been called his temple vision. He is transported to the temple, where he sees idol worship taking place in gross form. God promises to act in wrath against those who worshiped idols. And while God will pour out His wrath on Israel, He will pour all His wrath on Jesus on the cross. Jesus took all of the punishment for sin on the cross. Because Jesus took the wrath of God, we have rest from the wrath of God. How precious and sweet the gift of salvation is!

ROMANS 6:23 SAYS, "FOR THE WAGES OF SIN IS DEATH, BUT THE GIFT OF GOD IS ETERNAL LIFE IN CHRIST JESUS OUR LORD." HOW HAS READING EZEKIEL DEEPENED YOUR UNDERSTANDING OF THESE VERSES?

LIST THREE TO FIVE PEOPLE WHO YOU ARE PRAYING WOULD COME TO TRUST IN JESUS FOR SALVATION. TAKE A MOMENT TO PRAY FOR EACH OF THESE PEOPLE TO REPENT.

LIST THREE TIMES YOU SAW GOD'S JUSTICE ON DISPLAY IN EZEKIEL 5–8. HOW DO THESE PASSAGES INCREASE YOUR UNDERSTANDING OF WHO GOD IS?

Ezekiel 9–12

EZEKIEL 9 CAN SEEM LIKE A HARSH CHAPTER OF SCRIPTURE AS WE READ ABOUT GOD'S JUDGMENT, BUT THE REALITY IS THAT THE CONSEQUENCE OF SIN IS DEATH.

Every breath we breathe on earth is a gift of mercy from the Lord because none of us deserve it. The people of Judah did not realize that God saw their sin and was preparing to act on it. God commanded seven angels to execute this judgment. One angel marked the foreheads of the faithful while the other six executed all who did not have the mark.

In Ezekiel 10, we find one of the most heartbreaking scenes of the entire book. The glory of the Lord left the temple because of the people's rampant idolatry and continual rejection of God. Ezekiel gives us a depiction of the throne chariot of God coming to the temple and its courts and filling it, and then slowly moving from space to space. Finally, God's glory fully departed. This slow departure of God's glory reveals to us that He did not want to leave quickly. He gave more and more opportunities for His people to repent, but they did not.

In chapter 11, we see Ezekiel instructed to prophesy against wicked leaders. As he did so, one of them died. Ezekiel was overwhelmed and wondered if the Lord was going to bring an end to the entire remnant of Israel. But God encouraged Ezekiel that He would take care of the remnant of Israel's people. The Lord's presence had left the temple, but for the remnant of the Lord, He would be their sanctuary (Ezekiel 11:16). In these chapters that are heavy with judgment, we find promises that will extend beyond Israel's present or even post-exilic period and far into the future for God's chosen people. The promise was that some would be cleansed of their sin; they would be given new hearts and would be part of the remnant that would eventually return to their land.

It is important to note that the glory of the Lord finally left through the eastern gate (Ezekiel 10:18–19). When His glory returns at the end of Ezekiel, He will enter again through the eastern gate (Ezekiel 43:1–4). We will later see Jesus enter through the eastern gate when He rides on a donkey into Jerusalem the week before His crucifixion. It is here that Jesus reminds His disciples that He is the King who has come for the people of God (Matthew 21:1–11). The glory of the Lord in the flesh will soon come to Jerusalem. Though the Lord's presence left His city and His judgment would be poured out for their sin, He would not leave forever. God always desires to dwell with His people. Jesus's arrival gives evidence to that.

In chapter 12, Ezekiel was told by God to perform a few more action sermons. As we learned yesterday, Ezekiel was already in Babylon in captivity, but by his actions, he was foretelling that God's people would be exiled. While Israel and some of Judah had already been captured and exiled, the capital city of Jerusalem did not fall until about a decade later. Ezekiel was likely prophesying the final collapse of Jerusalem.

God always desires to dwell with His people.

READ 2 CHRONICLES 7:12–22. THESE WERE THE LORD'S WORDS WHEN HIS GLORY FIRST FILLED THE TEMPLE. WHAT SIGNIFICANCE DO THESE VERSES HOLD IN LIGHT OF THE EVENTS OF TODAY'S READING?

IN EZEKIEL 11:19–20, GOD SAYS HE WILL REMOVE THE PEOPLE'S HEARTS OF STONE AND GIVE THEM HEARTS OF FLESH. NOW, READ 2 CORINTHIANS 5:17. HOW DOES ONE RECEIVE THIS NEW HEART?

TAKE A MOMENT TO SUMMARIZE WHAT WE HAVE READ SO FAR IN EZEKIEL. WHAT HAVE YOU LEARNED ABOUT YOURSELF FROM THIS BOOK SO FAR? WHAT HAVE YOU LEARNED ABOUT GOD?

Ezekiel 13–15

THESE THREE CHAPTERS OF EZEKIEL ARE MAINLY ABOUT THE FALSE PROPHETS OF JUDAH.

These false prophets spoke as if they had a word from the Lord, but they did not. The false prophets ignored the truth and only said what sounded good to the people. They preached peace when disaster was soon to come. Like trying to whitewash a rotting building with a fresh coat of paint, they tried to make the people feel better about their sin, but this could not cure their unrighteousness. The people needed to be pushed to holiness—not given a pep talk.

The righteous remnant of God's people was able to see through the false prophets' wickedness, but the unrighteous easily went along with what they said. Just as Israel was divided over a message in Ezekiel 13, the message of the gospel also divides. Jesus's words reveal our broken condition and our need for His righteousness, yet there are many pastors and teachers who do not preach the divisive parts of Christ's message (Luke 12:49–53). Their avoidance is costly. The sin of man is great, and our need for the gospel is even greater. It is hard to hear how we are destined for sin without salvation from Christ, but the truth must be preached!

God reminds the people in Ezekiel 14 that He is bringing judgment because their hearts are full of idols. The Lord desired His people's hearts, and He knew that unless they faced judgment and suffering, they would continue to hold onto idols. Idolatry has been a repeated offense against God since the first sin of Adam and Eve. Every human born after them has dealt with idolatry and been guilty of it, as well. God continues to use suffering as a means of removing idols from the lives of His people. While suffering is not always a result of holding onto idols, it can reveal any idols we cling to instead of the Lord. The Lord desires all of our hearts. He is not satisfied with His people being divided in their worship.

Ezekiel 15 shows Israel as a useless vine because of her actions. Jesus will be the true Vine and the truer and better Israel. We will also be useless vines if we do not abide in Him. Apart from Christ, we can do nothing, so we must stay close to the Vine. We must abide in Him and allow Him to work in us. Abiding in Jesus means that we remain in Him and remember our union with Him (John 15). It is not another thing we have to do—it is a remembrance and gladness over our position in Christ. As we recognize our helplessness and are united with Christ, we are given all spiritual blessings and no longer need to look to idols to save us. Instead of looking to idols, we will only continue to love Jesus more and more.

> Apart from Christ, we can do nothing, so we must stay close to the Vine.

IN CHAPTER 13, EZEKIEL PROPHESIES AGAINST FALSE PROPHETS. THE ESV BIBLE SAYS THESE FALSE PROPHETS WERE PROPHESYING "FROM THEIR OWN HEARTS" (EZEKIEL 13:2).
What do you think this means? How can we be sure we are not living and speaking from our own hearts but according to the ways of God?

READ JOHN 15:1–8. HOW DOES THE VINE IN JOHN 15 DIFFER FROM THE VINE IN EZEKIEL 15?

JESUS SAYS THAT HE IS THE TRUE VINE IN JOHN 15:1. WHAT DO YOU THINK THIS MEANS IN LIGHT OF TODAY'S SCRIPTURE READING? WHAT DOES IT LOOK LIKE TO ABIDE IN THE VINE OF JESUS?

Ezekiel 13–15

Ezekiel 16–17

IN EZEKIEL 16 AND 17, EZEKIEL'S VIVID DESCRIPTIONS HELP US CLEARLY SEE HOW GOD'S PEOPLE WERE REJECTING HIM.

The Lord describes Israel as a baby cast out into a field and left to die. Israel was abandoned and unwanted, but the Lord chose to make her His own. He adorned her with beauty and entered into a covenant with her. He became her faithful husband. But Israel, His bride, was prideful in her beauty and status, and she committed adultery with foreign nations. She rejected the One who had saved her and loved her.

Israel would face discipline from her bridegroom for her wandering, but the Lord would remember His covenant with her. He would never abandon her and would not leave her to die. Instead, the Lord would deliver His bride from the shame of her sin. Ezekiel 16 is a picture of the gospel. We were the same as Israel, helpless and headed for death, but God redeemed us by the blood of Christ and brought us into His covenant family. May we never forget the Lord's faithfulness, and may we never put our trust in idols or worthless things that will never save us or love us as He will.

In Ezekiel 17, the Lord gives Ezekiel a riddle to speak to the house of Israel about two eagles and a vine. The riddle's purpose is to show the people the futility of trusting in anyone or anything other than the Lord. The first eagle represents King Nebuchadnezzar of Babylon. The top shoot of the cedar is King Jehoiachin, who ruled as the king of Judah until he was taken as an exile to Babylon by Nebuchadnezzar. The vine is Prince Zedekiah, who Nebuchadnezzar instated as a puppet king in the place of Jehoiachin. The second eagle is Pharaoh. Zedekiah was an unfaithful vine, and he put his trust in Pharaoh rather than the Lord's plans for Judah under the rule of Nebuchadnezzar. Zedekiah's decisions would ultimately lead to his death and the deaths of his entire family. Unlike Zedekiah, Christ will be a faithful Vine who will be obedient to the will of His Father. His faithfulness to the will of the Lord will lead to salvation for all who believe in Him. Jesus will fulfill the Lord's promise of a small twig that will be planted on top of a mountain and become a tree in which every bird can dwell. We will rest in the Righteous Branch and find our dwelling place in Him.

> God redeemed us by the blood of Christ and brought us into His covenant family.

EZEKIEL 16:1–14 TELLS THE STORY OF THE GOSPEL. LIST ALL OF THE THINGS GOD DOES FOR THE CHILD WHO WAS LEFT FORGOTTEN IN THE FIELD, AND NOTE THE LAVISH LOVE OF GOD.

EZEKIEL 16:15–43 TELLS A STORY ABOUT IDOLATRY. THE WOMAN CHASES OTHER LOVERS WHO END UP BEING HER DEMISE. IN YOUR OWN LIFE, WHAT HAPPENS WHEN YOU TRUST IN OTHER PEOPLE, YOURSELF, OR YOUR LIFE CIRCUMSTANCES INSTEAD OF IN GOD?

In contrast, what happens when you trust and pursue God wholeheartedly?

READ EZEKIEL 17:24. WHAT WORDS IN THIS VERSE DESCRIBE THE SOVEREIGNTY OF THE LORD? WHAT DO YOU LEARN ABOUT GOD FROM THIS VERSE?

Ezekiel 16–17

Ezekiel 18–19

IN EZEKIEL 18, THE PEOPLE OF GOD ASSUME THEY ARE SUFFERING, NOT BECAUSE OF THEIR OWN SIN BUT BECAUSE OF THE SINS OF PREVIOUS GENERATIONS.

Throughout these verses, God corrects their false understanding of obedience and grace. He is quick to remind them that every life belongs to Him (Ezekiel 18:4). In turn, they are quick to accuse God of being unfair in His judgments. God proves them wrong as He turns the attention back on them and their unjust ways (Ezekiel 18:25). God makes it clear that He is not the one at fault. Rather, their disobedience brought them to this low point.

This chapter concludes with God calling His people to "repent and live" (Ezekiel 18:32). If His people confessed and repented of their sin and looked to Him for redemption, God would be faithful to provide it. The same call of repentance is given to us today. If we turn from our sin, we receive redemption through the person of Christ. We are given new hearts. He is ready to receive all who will return to Him. Sadly, Israel would choose not to return to Him.

Ezekiel 19 contains a lament full of allegory, displaying the Lord's grief over the failure of Israel's leadership. The kings of Israel had failed miserably and fallen into sin. The latter half of the chapter is seen as a lament specifically over the Davidic kingdom, which would end at the reign of Zedekiah. Though the kingdom was "fruitful and full of branches" (Ezekiel 19:10), it would soon be uprooted and destroyed (Ezekiel 19:12–14).

The people of Israel had always put their hope in God's promise to continue David's line as they awaited the coming Messiah. However, they abused this promise of future deliverance to justify their present sin. They thought that because God told David He would establish His throne forever, they would not face serious consequences for disobeying Him. But the people were wrong. The line of David would come to a bitter end, and God's judgment would be brought against Judah. However, one day, a Son of David would come to deliver His people as a righteous and trustworthy King—this would be the Messiah, the One for whom they had been waiting. King Jesus reigns now and forever.

> One day, a Son of David would come to deliver His people as a righteous and trustworthy King.

HOW DO THESE TWO CHAPTERS DEEPEN YOUR UNDERSTANDING OF SIN AND ITS CONSEQUENCES?

WHEN ARE YOU TEMPTED TO BELIEVE THAT GOD'S WAYS ARE UNJUST OR UNKIND? HOW DOES EZEKIEL 18 HELP YOU TO HAVE AN ETERNAL PERSPECTIVE?

BECAUSE OF ISRAEL'S ONGOING DISOBEDIENCE, THEIR UNDERSTANDING OF GRACE WAS CHEAPENED AND DISTORTED. WHEN DO YOU TEND TO HAVE A DISTORTED VIEW OF GOD'S GRACE?

Ezekiel 20–21

EZEKIEL 20 DETAILS BOTH ISRAEL'S CYCLES OF UNFAITHFULNESS AS WELL AS GOD'S PLAN FOR ISRAEL.

Though the location would change, their pattern remained the same: they received God's provision, rejected God's commands, and turned to a pagan way of living. The people rebelled while they were in Egypt (Ezekiel 20:1–9), the wilderness (Ezekiel 20:10–26), and the Promised Land (Ezekiel 20:27–32). Even exile did not deter them from worshiping false idols. They no longer resembled the chosen people of God, set apart from all the nations.

There is a repeated phrase we have seen throughout the book of Ezekiel, and we see it again here in this chapter: "Then you will know that I am the Lord" (Ezekiel 20:38). Everything God has done—and will do—is for the glory of His name and the joy of His people. These acts of judgment are meant to draw His people back to Himself. We are to remember God's faithfulness to us as we go through trials, especially when we experience discipline from our loving Father. Through His discipline, we grow in dependence and holiness (Hebrews 12:3–11).

In Ezekiel 21, the Lord instructs Ezekiel to tell Jerusalem that His sword is drawn and about to strike. Through his groaning, Ezekiel was to display a broken heart and bitter grief over Jerusalem. He would cry out and wail because of the Lord's coming judgment through Nebuchadnezzar. The Lord would use this Babylonian king to bring destruction to His own city. The Davidic line would seem lost once Nebuchadnezzar finished his conquest, but one day, an unexpected King would come. Jesus is the true and better King promised to Israel. He will hold all judgment in His hands, and He will draw His sword—the sword of the Spirit, the Word of God—to lead His people in truth (Ephesians 6:17).

Left to our own devices, we would respond like Israel, looking to the wisdom of the world. Thankfully, the Lord intervened, and He rescued us through the precious blood of Jesus. Our salvation is not our own doing but is accomplished through the atoning work of Christ. By His Spirit, He leads us in righteousness and provides a way out of continuing our cycle of rebellion. Look to Him today, and know that He is Lord.

> Everything God has done—and will do—is for the glory of His name and the joy of His people.

THE ISRAELITES LOOKED TO THE WORLD FOR THEIR VALUE AND SECURITY RATHER THAN THE LORD. HOW ARE YOU TEMPTED TO LOOK FOR VALUE APART FROM CHRIST?

GOD BROUGHT BLESSING AND JUDGMENT UPON HIS PEOPLE SO THEY WOULD KNOW THAT HE IS THE LORD. HOW CAN YOU REMEMBER THAT HE IS THE LORD AS YOU GO THROUGH TRIALS, SUFFERING, OR DISCIPLINE?

HOW DOES READING THE BOOKS OF THE PROPHETS, LIKE EZEKIEL, HELP YOU UNDERSTAND THE PURPOSE OF GOD'S JUDGMENT?

Ezekiel 22–23

THESE CHAPTERS SHOW THE TERRIBLE DEPTHS OF ISRAEL'S SIN AND THE CONSEQUENCES THEY WILL ENDURE BECAUSE OF IT.

After all that the Lord had done for them, they continued to turn away from Him. Leaders neglected to lead the people in the way of the Lord. The nation was marked by injustice, idolatry, greed, lust, and even killing their children as sacrifices to idols. God's people had bent their morality and conscience to the evil world around them. Matters were only made worse by false prophets who made the people feel fine about their sin and claimed to have heard from the Lord when they had not (Ezekiel 22:25–26).

The Lord would show Judah and the world His wrath toward sin, even if it meant destroying His own city. The book of Ezekiel gives us just a glimpse into the absolute and holy wrath of God. Our sin is just as deserving of punishment as the sins of Israel and Judah. The penalty of sin must be paid through a perfect sacrifice. Jesus lived a perfectly holy life on our behalf and took on the wrath of God as He hung on the cross. The wrath that we should have experienced was poured out on our perfect Savior instead.

In chapter 23, Ezekiel presents an allegory of two women named Oholah and Oholibah. Oholah represents Samaria in the northern kingdom of Israel, and her story is marked with habitual sin and unfaithfulness. Because of her wickedness, she is given over to the hands of her enemies. Oholah's story is a warning that should be heeded by her sister, Oholibah. This sister represents Jerusalem in the southern kingdom of Judah. Though Oholibah witnessed the downfall of her sister, she refused to change her ways. Judgment is upon Judah for being stubborn and knowingly disobedient.

As we read the history of God's people, it can be easy to judge them for their decisions. But sadly, we often mirror their sinful and forgetful ways, turning away from the Lord to go after things of this world. We are like these sisters who have forgotten their first love. Mercifully, we have a faithful and loving bridegroom in Jesus. He saved us and clothed us with His robes of righteousness. We are invited to the marriage feast as His beloved bride, purified and redeemed through His sacrificial love (Revelation 19:6–9).

> The wrath that we should have experienced was poured out on our perfect Savior instead.

HOW CAN YOU REFLECT ON GOD'S FAITHFULNESS TODAY?

IN WHAT WAYS ARE YOU TEMPTED TO FORGET THE GOODNESS OF JESUS BY GOING AFTER THINGS OF THIS WORLD? HOW DOES EZEKIEL 23 CHALLENGE YOU TO PURSUE HOLINESS?

IF YOU ARE IN CHRIST, HE HAS SPARED YOU FROM EXPERIENCING HIS WRATH BECAUSE OF YOUR SIN. SPEND TIME PRAISING THE LORD FOR THAT TRUTH, AND PRAY FOR THOSE WHO DO NOT YET KNOW HIS SAVING GRACE.

Ezekiel 24–27

EZEKIEL 24 IS A MAJOR TURNING POINT IN THE BOOK AS EZEKIEL NOTES THAT NEBUCHADNEZZAR HAS FINALLY LAID SIEGE TO JERUSALEM.

God's people believed that they were safe, for they considered themselves to be the choice meat in the cooking pot of Ezekiel's vision. Instead, they would be poured out into the fire, consumed at the hand of Nebuchadnezzar with nothing remaining. The chapter ends with the death of Ezekiel's wife (Ezekiel 24:15–27). Ezekiel has been in the role of a mourner; now, he is commanded by God not to mourn outwardly, illustrating how the people will experience the demise of their beloved Jerusalem. Our God is a God of justice, and He would not let sin go unpunished. We must be vigilant for justice and reject idolatry. In a world that is ever-changing and easily swayed, we must stand for truth and cling to the only unchanging One.

In chapters 25–27, we see God's judgment for the neighboring nations, especially those who delighted in the destruction of Jerusalem. Even in His judgment, God desires the nations to turn to Him. Edom's fate represents those who are hardened in their sin and never turn to the Lord. Though some will never accept the gospel, we should be encouraged that Jesus will draw men and women from every nation to Himself.

These nations scoffed at God and built nations on their strength alone. Some, like Tyre, set themselves up as being great, yet the Lord would use Nebuchadnezzar to humble them. The people in Tyre are often associated with those who reject God. Their end is a pit of destruction in the world below. We were once among these people, headed to the same pit, but God intervened on our behalf and transferred us from death to life. In Christ, we inherit "the land of the living" (Ezekiel 26:20).

Ezekiel 27 shows the Lord asking Ezekiel to lament for Tyre, as one would do at a funeral. The utter rejection of the Lord is devastating to witness. God does not desire that anyone should perish but that all men would come to know Him (2 Peter 3:9). May we pursue those who do not yet know the Lord—that they would come to a saving faith in Christ and experience the freedom and joy that come from the beauty of the gospel.

> Jesus will draw men and women from every nation to Himself.

WHY WERE THESE NATIONS JUDGED BY GOD?

HOW DO THESE CHAPTERS CHALLENGE YOU IN YOUR RELATIONSHIPS WITH NONBELIEVERS?

TYRE'S PRIDE AND SELF-RELIANCE APART FROM GOD LED TO ITS DEMISE. HOW SHOULD WE LIVE DIFFERENTLY IN LIGHT OF THE GOSPEL?

Ezekiel 24–27

Ezekiel 28–31

FROM THE LEADERS OF TYRE TO THE PHARAOH OF EGYPT, THESE CHAPTERS FOCUS ON THE SIN OF PRIDE AND THE FATE OF THOSE WHO ARE FOREVER LOST TO ITS GRIP.

The Eden imagery used in the lament over the King of Tyre in Ezekiel 28 causes us to reflect on the moment when sin first entered the garden. Adam and Eve rejected God's rule that was implemented for their good. Thus, they were exiled from their home and experienced death. Christ came as the second Adam who perfectly obeyed God's commands and secured eternal life for His people. Where the first Adam failed, the second Adam succeeded (Romans 5:12–21).

The rest of today's chapters detail prophecies against Egypt, continuing the theme of pride leading to the downfall of the wicked. Both the rulers of Tyre and Egypt set themselves up as gods to be worshiped. They attributed what came from the hand of God as coming from themselves and their gods. Even Pharaoh claimed to have made the Nile himself. All of these nations, however, were under the power of Almighty God. After Babylon destroyed Egypt, Egypt would never control the nations of the world in the same way again (Ezekiel 29:15, 19).

Egypt was an old enemy of Israel who enslaved them for hundreds of years. Though God had delivered them, Israel repeatedly returned to Egypt. The Lord would demonstrate once more to His people—and to Egypt—that false gods could do nothing for them (Ezekiel 30:13). In Ezekiel 31, we again see imagery from Eden as we learn that Pharaoh will meet his end. Just like the king of Tyre, his nation will face destruction.

Though we have placed our faith in Christ, we often forget the beauty of the gospel; instead, we are tempted to trust in ourselves and the idols of the world. God shows us that these idols can do nothing for us and that Christ will ultimately destroy each and every one. We must be careful to not allow ourselves to be filled with prideful attitudes that lead to idolizing ourselves and the world (Romans 12:3). Pride can sneak into our lives very subtly, and we must always be on guard against it. When we remember who we are in light of God and His promises, we can walk in humility and gratitude, knowing that all we have comes from our Father.

> We can walk in humility and gratitude, knowing that all we have comes from our Father.

READ ROMANS 5:12–21. WHAT DOES IT MEAN THAT CHRIST IS THE SECOND ADAM? WHAT DOES THIS MEAN FOR YOU TODAY?

HOW CAN REFLECTING ON GOD'S PROMISES KEEP YOU FROM PRIDE?

WHAT IDOLS OF THE WORLD COMPETE FOR YOUR ALLEGIANCE?

Ezekiel 32–34

EZEKIEL 32 CONTINUES WITH YET ANOTHER PROPHECY AGAINST EGYPT THROUGH THE FORM OF A LAMENT.

This has been a common theme as Ezekiel mourns the death and destruction he is called to pronounce to the nations. The Lord gives Ezekiel a horrific description of Pharaoh's demise in this chapter. Pharaoh's death points to the greater destruction of Egypt and those who have rejected God—they will be utterly ravaged and destroyed. The depiction of Pharaoh's destroyed corpse is a contrast to a later passage in Ezekiel that depicts the regeneration God offers to those who follow Him. Bones are resurrected with flesh and new hearts. The bones of those who rebel against God will never experience this. Jesus will be victorious over the princes of the world, providing new life to those who seek Him. He is the true King who brings His people into peace with God.

Chapter 33 begins the last section of the book, in which the prophet brings words of hope and restoration to Israel. We see Ezekiel pictured as a watchman for Israel. The people would have been familiar with this role—a watchman was tasked with standing on the city wall to warn of danger. Ezekiel's message of repentance is one for us to share today, warning the world of the consequences of their sin and pointing them to hope and restoration found in Jesus.

Ezekiel 33:21 is a critical moment in this narrative, as Ezekiel receives news that Jerusalem has finally fallen. God has done what He said He would do, and His judgment would be thorough. Ezekiel 33 is a sobering reminder that one day it will be too late for repentance, and judgment will be set. This truth should urge us to share the gospel, knowing that the Lord will reveal the truth to those He has called.

Chapter 34 displays the incredible faithfulness of our God, who will never neglect His children. The shepherds, or leaders, of Israel had let the people down and led them astray. Their selfishness had allowed for the spiritual decay of the city and its ultimate destruction. Now, God would rescue His people and be their Shepherd. Ezekiel 34:23–24 contains a promise referring to a King who would come from the line of David. This is Jesus, our Good Shepherd. No longer slaves to darkness, our future is one of eternal peace, full of beauty and hope (Ezekiel 34:25–31).

God would rescue His people and be their Shepherd.

HOW DO CHAPTERS 1–33 OF EZEKIEL HELP YOU APPRECIATE THE WORDS OF HOPE AND RESTORATION FOUND IN CHAPTER 34?

WHERE ARE YOU TEMPTED TO PLACE YOUR HOPE OTHER THAN JESUS?

HOW DOES REMEMBERING THAT JESUS IS OUR PERFECT KING ENCOURAGE YOU WHEN EARTHLY RULERS AND LEADERS DISAPPOINT YOU?

Ezekiel 32–34

Ezekiel 35–37

IN EZEKIEL 35, WE READ A PROPHECY AGAINST ISRAEL'S ENEMY, EDOM.

Because of their hatred toward Israel, God would destroy them. As Jerusalem was desolate after the Babylonian destruction, Edom will also be. But the mountains of Jerusalem had a much different fate than the current situation they faced. Ezekiel 36 paints a beautiful picture of how they would be restored to their former glory. The Lord promised to bring life back to their land.

Ezekiel 36:24–30 shows how God intends to restore His people. He will bring them out of exile and back to their land. He will cleanse them of their sin and give them a new heart. God will place His Spirit within them so they can obey Him. Their identity will be God's chosen people, and He will be their one true God. He was faithful to do this for Israel's remnant, and if we are in Christ, He has done this for us as well. He changes people from the inside out by giving them His Spirit. Once we have encountered Him, we will never be the same. Our God changes everything.

Our God brings dead things to life (Romans 4:17). All of Scripture points to this glorious truth. God brought Ezekiel to a valley of dry bones to show the prophet the current spiritual condition of Israel. Before Ezekiel lay an entire valley full of bones that, by man's standards, were useless. But as Ezekiel spoke God's active word to them and prophesied the breath of God over them, the impossible became a reality as the dry bones came to life (Ezekiel 37:10, Hebrews 4:12). Our God can give life to what was once dead. This is the power of His Word. He can turn the hearts of His people back to Himself.

After the bones come to life, the scene shifts to the future, and we are given a picture of our beautiful inheritance through the gospel. Jesus is the perfect King who God promises at the end of this chapter, and He will be our King forever (Ezekiel 37:24–25). The Lord will give His people an everlasting covenant of peace, and He will dwell with us forever (Ezekiel 37:26–27). God will forever be faithful to His people. This is the hope we have in Christ.

> God will forever be faithful to His people. This is the hope we have in Christ.

GOD PROVIDES RESTORATION TO HIS PEOPLE BY GIVING THEM A NEW HEART AND HIS SPIRIT. HOW IS THE HOLY SPIRIT AT WORK IN YOU TODAY? ARE THERE AREAS IN YOUR LIFE WHERE YOU NEED RESTORATION?

GOD HAS THE POWER TO GIVE LIFE TO WHAT WAS ONCE DEAD. HOW DOES THIS ENCOURAGE YOU AS YOU ENCOUNTER PEOPLE WHO HAVE HARD HEARTS TOWARD THE GOSPEL?

HOW HAVE YOU EXPERIENCED THE POWER OF GOD'S WORD IN YOUR LIFE?

Ezekiel 35–37

Ezekiel 38–39

THESE TWO CHAPTERS OF EZEKIEL CAN BE DIFFICULT TO DECIPHER AS WE ARE INTRODUCED TO A RULER NAMED GOG.

This name only appears in a couple of places in Scripture, but Genesis 10 may provide some helpful context. In a passage known as the Table of Nations, Genesis 10 shows us the names of the various people groups that would spread throughout the ancient world. The places mentioned here in Ezekiel 38 are all represented in this list of nations, including Magog (Genesis 10:2), which is translated as "land of Gog." Since Gog is allied with several foreign nations (Ezekiel 38:2–3, 5–6), it is likely that this ruler is a representation of Israel's foreign enemies, a picture of human rebellion against a holy God.

We see Ezekiel use vivid imagery as he describes the defeat of Gog and his army. Bloodshed, fire, and an earthquake are among the many devastations that they will experience as a result of God's wrath. The conclusion of this chapter helps point us to God's purpose in executing judgment—revealing Himself through His greatness and holiness so that the nations would know that He is the Lord (Ezekiel 38:23).

Ezekiel 39 continues to describe the defeat of Gog with even more graphic detail. This sets the stage for the Lord to remind His people that He will always reign victorious over His enemies. The people endured great hardship in exile because of their own rebellion, but God's compassion will bring them back to a restored relationship with Him. The Lord promises that He will be their defense. His face is no longer hidden from them (Ezekiel 39:23), for He will always be with them. And God's purposes in their judgment remain the same in their restoration—so that they will know that He is the Lord their God (Ezekiel 39:22, 28).

Ezekiel's vision in these chapters reminds us how the people of God will continue to face trials, persecution, discipline, and suffering. But God will remain faithful as He defeats the enemies of His people (Revelation 20:8–9). No enemy rivals the power of the Lord, and we can be confident in our great Savior who has conquered evil and death. Chapters 38–39 encourage us to remember that evil will never thwart the promises of God.

> We can be confident in our great Savior who has conquered evil and death.

HOW IS GOD'S PRESENCE A COMFORT TO YOU AS YOU FACE TIMES OF HARDSHIP OR SUFFERING?

**WHAT IS THE MAIN POINT OF THESE TWO CHAPTERS IN EZEKIEL?
HOW IS IT SIGNIFICANT FOR THE FUTURE OF ISRAEL?**

HOW IS GOD'S CHARACTER ON DISPLAY AS HE DESCRIBES ISRAEL'S EVENTUAL RESTORATION?

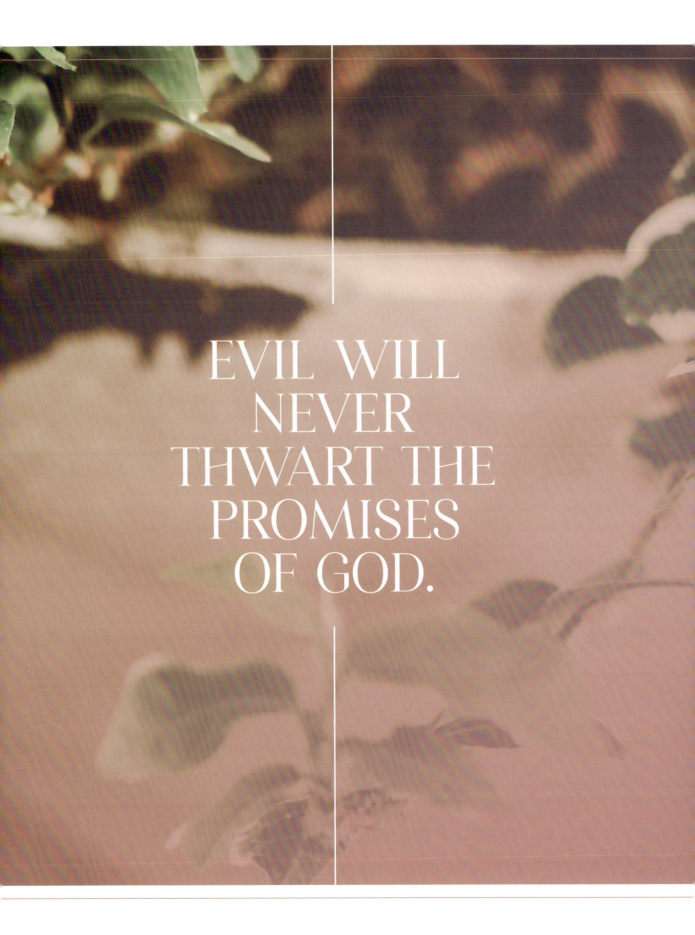

Ezekiel 40-41

THE END OF THE BOOK OF EZEKIEL LOOKS TO THE FUTURE AND THE RESTORATION OF GOD'S PEOPLE.

Ezekiel 40 starts a series of chapters that will conclude this prophetic book. Fourteen years after the destruction of Jerusalem, the Lord gives Ezekiel a vision of the reconstruction of the temple. There are many opinions among scholars about whether this is a literal or figurative temple. The detail of the descriptions can lead one to believe that it is a literal temple. However, it is difficult to know for sure. Regardless of how you interpret this vision, these chapters point to God's majestic holiness and the necessity for us to worship Him.

As a priest, Ezekiel would have been familiar with the details of the temple. But after the destruction of Jerusalem, he was now experiencing it in a new way. He was seeing God's restoration at work through this vision. While the details in these chapters can be overwhelming, imagine how this would have comforted those in exile, mourning the loss of the temple. Through this vision, God's people were assured that their temple would be restored, and He would dwell with them once again.

In Ezekiel 41, the prophet continues to provide details about the temple and focuses on the inner places. It is important to note that Ezekiel includes descriptions of carved images of cherubim and palm trees as being on the temple's walls (Ezekiel 41:18). These images are considered to be signs of protection, as seen in the garden of Eden. When Adam and Eve were banished from their home, God placed cherubim and a flaming sword to guard the Tree of Life (Genesis 3:24).

God first dwelled with His people in the garden, and now He dwells within us through the Holy Spirit (2 Corinthians 6:16). The temple has always pointed us back to the first dwelling place in Eden, and it also represents the future world that the people of God will inhabit for all of eternity. Rather than the glory of God filling a physical temple, His glory will be poured out over all of creation. Creation will finally reach its consummation, and God will dwell with His people forever (Revelation 21).

> These chapters point to God's majestic holiness and the necessity for us to worship Him.

HOW DO THESE CHAPTERS COMPEL YOU TO WORSHIP THE LORD?

WHAT CONNECTIONS CAN YOU MAKE BETWEEN THE TEMPLE AND THE GARDEN OF EDEN?

READ 2 CORINTHIANS 6:16. HOW CAN EZEKIEL 40–41 HELP YOU REFLECT ON GOD DWELLING WITHIN YOU?

Ezekiel 42–44

IN EZEKIEL 42, THE VISION OF THE NEW TEMPLE CONTINUES WITH A DETAILED DESCRIPTION OF THE PRIESTS' CHAMBERS AND THE TEMPLE COMPLEX.

With each measurement and detail of the temple, we see God's sovereign intentionality in restoring the place where His people would come to worship Him. Though God's people have been exiled for their disobedience, this vision reminds them of His power to rebuild and restore what was once lost.

At the beginning of Ezekiel, God's presence sadly left the temple. In Ezekiel 43, His presence gloriously returns and will never leave His people again. Ezekiel describes the voice of the Lord like the roar of rushing waters, and He writes that the earth shone with His glory. In Revelation, similar imagery is used to describe the sound of Christ's voice (Revelation 1:15) and how God's glory illuminates the earth (Revelation 21:23). God is powerful and holy, and He is taking His rightful place in the temple. He is the one true God worthy of all honor, glory, and praise. The purpose in giving Ezekiel this vision is to bring about repentance—for the people of God to turn from their sin and turn toward the Lord in joyful obedience.

Though the people had sinned against God, God made a way for them to return to Him. In Ezekiel 44, God makes it clear that the outer gate is to remain closed. This points to God's holiness, for no one else is to enter through it after Him. It also emphasizes the permanence of His presence, for He will not leave His people. Jesus's second coming in Revelation will signal our being brought into the presence of God forever. The Lord will never leave us or forsake us—we will worship in His presence for all eternity.

The end of chapter 44 reminds us that the Levitical priests do not inherit land or possessions. Instead, God is their inheritance, and their provision comes from Him alone. In Christ, we have a glorious inheritance (Ephesians 1:14, 1 Peter 1:3–9). In this world, we will face opposition, loss, and suffering, but our eternal inheritance in Christ is secure. It will never diminish or be taken away. There is something so much better to come for the people of God.

> Though the people had sinned against God, God made a way for them to return to Him.

HOW WOULD YOU SUMMARIZE THE PURPOSE FOR THE VISION OF THE NEW TEMPLE?
HOW DOES THIS INFORM HOW YOU READ THESE CHAPTERS?

READ EPHESIANS 1:14. ACCORDING TO THIS VERSE, WHAT ROLE DOES THE HOLY SPIRIT PLAY IN OUR ETERNAL INHERITANCE? HOW DOES THIS HELP YOU DEVELOP AN ETERNAL PERSPECTIVE?

REFLECT ON THE GLORY OF GOD AS SEEN IN THIS PASSAGE.
HOW DOES REFLECTING ON THE MAJESTY OF GOD HELP YOU TO PURSUE HOLINESS?

Ezekiel 45–48

THE BOOK OF EZEKIEL IS FILLED WITH DECLARATIONS OF JUDGMENT FOR SIN AND PROMISES OF ULTIMATE REDEMPTION AND RESTORATION FOR GOD'S PEOPLE.

Our God is a God of justice, and He will punish evil. But His judgment does not come without promises of mercy and calls to return to the Lord. The book ends with the extraordinary vision of a future temple in which God's people will worship Him for His holiness and faithfulness through all generations. In this future time, every promise that God has made to His people will be fulfilled. These promises of hope outshine the hopelessness from the beginning of the book. The city of Jerusalem was destroyed, but God would allow His faithful remnant to see the new city they will dwell in forever. What a difference between the beginning of Ezekiel and the end of it!

In the last few chapters of Ezekiel, the prophet focuses on a figure called "the prince." It is likely that this prince is a reference to the coming Messiah, the fulfillment of the line of David, Jesus Christ. What is so interesting about the prince's actions is that He is responsible for all of the offerings the people give to the Lord (Ezekiel 45:13–17).

Later in redemptive history, we will see Jesus absolve the sacrificial system because He is the perfect and final sacrifice given for the sins of God's people. And the inheritance of this prince will belong to his sons and servants (Ezekiel 46:16–18). Through Christ's atoning work on the cross, He has allowed us to become children of the Most High God. Because of our union with Him, we are given His inheritance. We receive the righteousness of Jesus and favor with God. We will never be separated from Christ, and our future is secure in Him.

Just as the people of Israel who heard these prophecies only saw in part what was to come, we also only see in part. We wait for the day when we will see death and sin defeated and the completion of every promise at Christ's return. The Lord will keep every word of His promises, and we will be reminded of His sovereign hand and the treasure of redemption on the day when we are brought to our heavenly home to stay forever. For now, we wait in the tension of the "already and not yet," but someday, we will see every promise fulfilled.

> Someday, we will see every promise fulfilled.

SUMMARIZE THE MAIN POINT OF EZEKIEL.

HOW DOES EZEKIEL 47 POINT YOU TO THE ABUNDANT LIFE FOUND IN CHRIST?

REFLECT ON THE VERY LAST VERSE OF THE BOOK. CONSIDERING ALL THAT YOU LEARNED THROUGH EZEKIEL, WHY IS THIS A FITTING CONCLUSION?

Joel 1-3

THOUGH SHORT, THE BOOK OF JOEL GIVES BELIEVERS A SOBERING PICTURE OF GOD'S JUDGMENT WHILE ALSO PROVIDING A GLORIOUS GLIMPSE OF THE FUTURE.

Joel's prophecies have both near and far fulfillments, meaning Judah would experience some of them quickly while others would await fulfillment when Christ returns. Many scholars believe Joel's prophecies to Judah occurred shortly before the Babylonian invasion in 586 BC. For this reason, we will place Joel just after Ezekiel and just before Daniel.

In chapter 1, Joel urges the people to tell their children about the Lord so that they could carry the truth to each generation. We have seen this generational pattern urged in other places in Scripture as well. When the people did not remember the Lord and teach each new generation about Him, they soon turned to other gods and did whatever they pleased. This then required discipline. Joel describes a plague of locusts being carried out against Israel. This plague was both real and symbolic as Joel calls Judah to repent. If the people did not repent, then an army like this plague of locusts would bring judgment on the day of the Lord—a judgment far worse than any plague.

The first fulfillment of this fateful day comes at the hand of a foreign nation that would invade Judah, but the ultimate fulfillment of the day of the Lord is yet to come. As seen in the book of Revelation, the coming day of the Lord will be when Christ returns, accompanied by His heavenly army, to set up His kingdom (Joel 2:2). Joel indicates through a rhetorical question that no one without Christ can endure the day of the Lord. Without the righteous work of Christ on the cross, the day of the Lord brings great hopelessness. But because we are united with Christ, this day will bring us great joy.

The Lord does not leave the people in hopelessness. He tells them to return to Him, and He will restore them. Our repentance and restoration are only possible because of the salvation provided through Jesus. Joel even describes the day of Pentecost when the Holy Spirit was poured out onto the people of God (Joel 2:28–32). The final verses of Joel end with Jesus dwelling and reigning over Jerusalem. We will dwell in the house of the Lord because of Christ. Though our sin is as great as the people of Israel, God provides restoration through Jesus, and we joyfully await the day we will dwell with Him in the new heaven and new earth.

> We will dwell in the house of the Lord because of Christ.

THOUGH JOEL'S MESSAGE OF JUDGMENT IS NECESSARY AND DIFFICULT, HOW DOES IT POINT US TO CHRIST AND GIVE US HOPE AS WELL?

READ JOEL 2:12–13. WHAT DO YOU NEED TO TURN FROM AND SEEK REPENTANCE FOR? HOW DO THE ATTRIBUTES OF GOD IN THESE VERSES GIVE YOU ASSURANCE HE WILL WELCOME YOU BACK WITH OPEN ARMS?

READ EZEKIEL 37:27–28. HOW ARE EZEKIEL AND JOEL'S PROPHECIES SIMILAR? TO WHAT GREAT TIME DO THEY REFER?

Daniel 1–3

THE ACCOUNT OF DANIEL BEGINS DURING THE TIME OF ISRAEL'S EXILE AS SEVERAL YOUNG MEN ARE CARRIED OFF INTO CAPTIVITY IN BABYLON.

Daniel is one of the first deportees from Jerusalem. The noble young men are brought into the king's court and are taught the pagan ways of the Babylonians, who are also sometimes referred to as the Chaldeans. In Daniel 2, Nebuchadnezzar has a troubling dream. He gathers the wisest men in the land and gives them an impossible task—they must tell the dream he had and interpret its meaning. If they cannot follow through, they will be put to death. The men tell him that there is no one alive who could do as the king requests, but this only infuriates him more. Nebuchadnezzar orders all wise men in the land to be executed, including Daniel and his friends.

When Daniel hears of this, he seeks the Lord, and the Lord faithfully reveals Nebuchadnezzar's vision to him. Even in the wisest of men, human wisdom is limited, but God's wisdom never ends. He is the source of all wisdom. Daniel gives God credit for revealing Nebuchadnezzar's vision to him and its interpretation. The vision shows that there are kingdoms coming that will surpass Babylon, but they will be nothing compared to the kingdom of God. Because of Daniel's interpretation, he is promoted as ruler over the city of Babylon, and Daniel promotes his friends as well.

Daniel 3 is a familiar story in which Daniel's three friends refuse to worship an idol made by Nebuchadnezzar. Nebuchadnezzar realizes that the God of Israel is powerful, but he still does not claim Him as the one true God. Nebuchadnezzar's decision to cast these three men into the fire for their refusal to worship his idol will only be another opportunity for the Lord to display His power and authority over all false gods. When the Lord saves Daniel's friends from the fire, Nebuchadnezzar worships God, but he still does not follow Him.

In this foreign land, Daniel and his friends will demonstrate their faithfulness to the Lord, but more importantly, God will demonstrate His faithfulness to His people. God blessed Daniel and his friends with health, strength, and wisdom as they served in Nebuchadnezzar's court. They were an example to a watching world as they followed God above all else. In Christ, we have been given all spiritual blessings (Ephesians 1:3), and God calls us to demonstrate those blessings to the world around us.

> Human wisdom is limited, but God's wisdom never ends. He is the source of all wisdom.

HOW CAN YOU PURSUE WISDOM FROM THE LORD RATHER THAN THE WISDOM THAT THE WORLD OFFERS?

WHAT ASPECTS OF GOD'S CHARACTER ARE ON DISPLAY IN THESE CHAPTERS?

DANIEL'S FRIENDS WERE OBEDIENT, EVEN IN THE FACE OF DEATH.
HOW DOES THIS CHALLENGE YOU IN YOUR PURSUIT OF WHOLEHEARTED OBEDIENCE TO THE LORD?

Daniel 4-6

IN DANIEL 4, WE SEE THAT NEBUCHADNEZZAR—WHO, AT THE TIME, WAS THE MIGHTIEST KING IN THE WORLD—IS SHOUTING THE PRAISES OF GOD IN RESPONSE TO DANIEL'S INTERPRETATION.

And yet, Nebuchadnezzar asks Daniel to interpret another one of his dreams because "a spirit of the holy gods is in him" (Daniel 4:8). Daniel makes it very clear that the Lord is the one true God who works within him, but Nebuchadnezzar still does not see the truth.

Nebuchadnezzar's dream depicts a large and beautiful tree that is strong and fruitful, but then he dreams that this tree will be cast away and destroyed. Daniel tells Nebuchadnezzar that he is the tree. Nebuchadnezzar will set himself up as higher than God in his own eyes, and the Lord will bring him low. It is finally in Nebuchadnezzar's humiliation that he calls upon the Lord in repentance, and the Lord restores him. The narrative immediately moves on to the reign of the next king, Belshazzar. Belshazzar is full of the passion and lust of the world. He did not learn from his predecessor by humbling himself before God. However, the Lord will quickly judge Belshazzar and bring an end to his kingdom.

At Belshazzar's feast, a hand mysteriously appears and writes on the wall (Daniel 5:5–12). When Daniel reveals what the message means, Belshazzar tries to cover up his wrongdoing by honoring Daniel and giving him authority in the kingdom that Daniel knows is about to fall. Belshazzar is killed that very night. The lives of Nebuchadnezzar and Belshazzar remind us that there are two responses we can have to the message of the gospel—either we repent and receive new life, or we rebel and continue toward spiritual death.

The Babylonian kingdom will fall to the Medes and Persians, and Darius the Mede will be the next king Daniel will serve under. In chapter 6, Daniel continues to succeed and is favored by this new king because of the wisdom God gives him. God consistently provides for Daniel, even when he is thrown into a lion's den for his worship of the Lord. Our allegiance to Jesus will bring glory to His name. Persecution of the saints brings an opportunity for others to hear the gospel. When Daniel leaves the lion's den, Darius, a pagan king, praises the God of Israel. Because of stories like Daniel's, we can trust in the Lord, for Jesus is our deliverer.

Our allegiance to Jesus will bring glory to His name.

IN WHAT WAYS DOES DANIEL DISPLAY HIS DEPENDENCE ON GOD?
HOW CAN YOU DEEPEN YOUR DEPENDENCE ON THE LORD TODAY?

HOW DOES THE STORY OF DANIEL ENCOURAGE YOU TO TRUST GOD IN ALL CIRCUMSTANCES?

WHAT SIMILARITIES AND DIFFERENCES DO YOU SEE IN NEBUCHADNEZZAR AND BELSHAZZAR?

Daniel 7–9

DANIEL 7 INTRODUCES A SIGNIFICANT SHIFT IN THE STORY.

The book moves from Daniel's life in Babylon to the recording of Daniel's dreams and prophecy of future events. It can be confusing to read prophetic literature like this, but we must keep in mind the big picture of these passages as we read. These visions remind us of the Lord's sovereignty throughout all of time and history. Ultimately, we see that God will be victorious over His enemies.

In Daniel's first vision, he witnesses a battle between worldly kingdoms and the kingdom of heaven. Daniel sees the worldly kingdoms as four beasts, but they are overshadowed as the Lord, the Ancient of Days, takes a seat on His throne (Daniel 7:9). Then, Daniel sees a figure who is "like a son of man" yet divine in nature (Daniel 7:13). He is given eternal dominion, and His rule will have no end. Throughout His earthly ministry, Jesus likely had this passage in mind as He referred to Himself as the Son of Man. Daniel 7 is a beautiful reminder of how Jesus brings hope amid chaos. Though our world is constantly changing, we can take comfort in knowing that Jesus will ultimately reign forever. Daniel's visions continue in chapter 8. As the Lord gives him these visions, Daniel is alarmed at what he sees. The consistent theme is that God rules over all and will be victorious in the end. Every event in the world around us has been ordained and purposed by the Lord.

As Daniel reads Jeremiah's prophecy about the seventy years that the people would be in exile, Daniel goes before the Lord in sackcloth to pray and weep for his people. The people have been faithless to the Lord, but He has always been faithful to them. Daniel's prayer in chapter 9 is a beautiful picture of our hope in the gospel. We do not rely on our righteousness before God but on His great mercy displayed toward us through Christ. The angel Gabriel comes to Daniel to help him understand. He explains what the restoration of Jerusalem will soon look like and touches on its eventual destruction. Gabriel also reminds Daniel that he is treasured by God (Daniel 9:23). We, too, are tenderly loved by God, and through the work of Jesus, we can share His love with a world that desperately needs it.

> These visions remind us of the Lord's sovereignty throughout all of time and history.

WHAT CLUES ARE PROVIDED TO INDICATE THE SHIFT FROM NARRATIVE TO PROPHETIC LITERATURE? WHY IS IT IMPORTANT TO KEEP GENRE IN MIND AS YOU READ GOD'S WORD?

WHAT ELEMENTS OF DANIEL'S PRAYER IN CHAPTER 9 CAN YOU TAKE AND APPLY TO YOUR OWN PRAYER LIFE?

GOD SENDS GABRIEL TO REMIND DANIEL OF HIS LOVE FOR HIM. HOW HAS GOD DISPLAYED HIS LOVE TOWARD YOU?

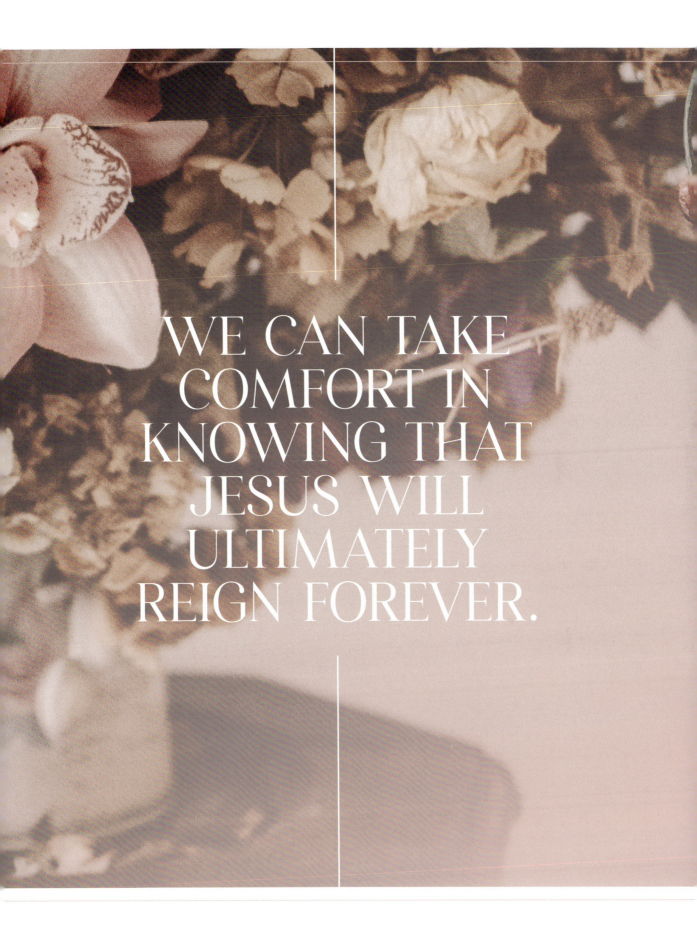

Daniel 10-12

THE FINAL CHAPTERS OF DANIEL CONTAIN ONE MORE VISION.

As Daniel witnesses the spiritual realm, we remember that there are unseen spiritual battles around us, as well (Daniel 10:18–21, Ephesians 6:12). An angelic being appears to Daniel, strengthening him and reminding him that he is greatly loved by God. But as Daniel listens, he learns that there are spiritual beings who fight for the people of God. Though it can be overwhelming to think about the things we cannot see, we have nothing to fear, for we have been given a great Savior who fights on our behalf.

Daniel 11 includes a unique prophecy detailing the future events of Greek and Persian kings. There is great debate among scholars about when this section was written, what kings are being described, and how we are to understand this prophecy. Though we may not know all the details, one thing we learn from this chapter is that God's people will continue to endure trials and hardship. We see that this is true even today. However, we do not need to be disheartened because we know that this world is not our forever home. Our hope lies in eternity—when Christ returns to establish His kingdom of which there will be no end.

Throughout this book, we see that Daniel was a man of purpose, prayer, humility, and conviction. As he lived in Babylon under pagan rule, the Lord gave him wisdom and discernment, as well as prophetic insight into future events and what lay ahead for God's people. Daniel got just a glimpse of the spiritual warfare at work in the world, but he was not paralyzed by it. Instead, he allowed it to push him further toward the Lord in prayer. Daniel lived in a time when his faith was ridiculed, yet he never let his faith in the Lord waver. There must have been many times when Daniel did not understand what was ahead, but he always turned to the Lord.

The prophecies in this book are valuable for us to read today because each one points us to a sovereign God who will keep His promises to His people. Daniel is encouraged to rest, knowing he will receive his eternal reward at the end of his life. Because of Christ's sacrifice, we have been given eternal peace and security. We can rest in Him, knowing that He goes before us in all things.

> Our hope lies in eternity—when Christ returns to establish His kingdom of which there will be no end.

HOW WOULD YOU SUMMARIZE THE TWO SECTIONS OF DANIEL (CHAPTERS 1–6 AND CHAPTERS 7–12)?

WHAT PART OF DANIEL'S STORY HAS CHALLENGED YOU THE MOST?

WHAT DOES IT LOOK LIKE TO REST IN CHRIST ALONE?

Ezra 1–3
Psalm 137

BEFORE WE BEGIN THE BOOK OF EZRA, IT IS IMPORTANT TO TAKE A MOMENT AND UNDERSTAND THE HEARTBREAK OF GOD'S PEOPLE AS THEY ENTERED EXILE.

In Psalm 137, the psalmist gives a picture of the people sitting on the great rivers of Babylon, mourning their losses and the horror they saw as their temple, homes, and families were destroyed. Their loss and pain were great, but they trusted God would vindicate them. It would be many years, but God's faithfulness to His people was sure, and the journey home begins in the book of Ezra.

After seventy years of captivity, the Lord used King Cyrus of Persia to make a proclamation that God's chosen people could return to Jerusalem and rebuild the temple. The book of Ezra chronicles this historic event as one of God's many promises was fulfilled, and restoration for the nation of Israel began. By stirring the heart of King Cyrus, God showed His sovereign control over all earthly rulers and His faithfulness to His covenants.

In chapter 1, Ezra records the message that King Cyrus received from the Lord. The king also returned all the temple articles that Nebuchadnezzar had taken when Jerusalem was destroyed by Babylon. King Cyrus had every last item returned to Sheshbazzar, the prince of Judah. Not only did the Lord restore the temple articles, but He also preserved a member of the royal line. Zerubbabel, who returned home with the exiles, was the governor of Judah (Haggai 1:1), a grandson of the former King Jehoiachin (who is also sometimes referred to as Jeconiah), and thus a descendant of David. As we have previously discussed, this was significant as this was the line of Judah from which the Messiah would come, just as God promised (Genesis 49:10). As the people gathered the temple articles, chapter 2 chronicles the descendants who returned to Jerusalem under the leadership of Sheshbazzar and Zerubbabel. The remnant was going home.

As the exiles returned home and resettled their homeland, the work of rebuilding began. It started with the rebuilding of the altar and the temple foundation for the worship of the Lord. As the foundation stones were laid, the people sang and gave thanks to the Lord as they sang, "For he is good; his faithful love to Israel endures forever" (Ezra 3:11). The people of Israel had long been unfaithful to the Lord, as is chronicled throughout the Old Testament. Yet despite His people's persistent unfaithfulness, the Lord did not neglect His promises.

Opposition abounds in the chapters ahead as we see God's people seek to resettle their homeland. We will also see God's sovereignty over the hearts of men continue, as He uses earthly kings to accomplish His divine plan. Nothing would thwart God's plan to bring His children home. The time had come for the next step in God's plan of salvation and redemption to begin.

IN WHAT WAYS DOES THE STORY OF THE EXILES' RETURN DEMONSTRATE THAT NO DETAIL IS TOO SMALL FOR GOD? HOW DOES THIS ENCOURAGE YOU IN YOUR OWN LIFE?

HOW DOES GOD'S SOVEREIGN POWER OVER KINGS AND KINGDOMS GIVE YOU HOPE AS YOU LIVE IN OUR CURRENT POLITICAL AND GLOBAL CLIMATE?

READ EZRA 3:11 AGAIN. TAKE SOME TIME TO RECORD KEY EVENTS IN ISRAEL'S HISTORY THAT DISPLAY GOD'S FAITHFULNESS TO ISRAEL OVER THE CENTURIES. THEN RECORD A PRAYER OF PRAISE FOR HIS FAITHFULNESS TO YOU.

Ezra 4–6

THE FOUNDATION OF THE TEMPLE WAS FRESHLY LAID; HOWEVER, IT DID NOT TAKE LONG FOR THE LOCAL INHABITANTS OF THE LAND TO BECOME ADVERSARIES.

Though they claimed to worship Yahweh (the Hebrew name for God), their evil schemes did not fool Zerubbabel. Chapter 4 records these schemes as the rebuilding efforts were opposed and halted completely for about fifteen years. The people were likely discouraged and confused. After all, they had returned to the Promised Land to do what God had called them to do, only to face opposition that stopped their work for the Lord.

But this was the Lord's work, and He would remain faithful to His remnant. He was sovereign over every part of the journey, including the opposition. He was not taken off guard or surprised by the difficulties they faced in their service to Him. The building eventually began again with the help of prophets like Haggai and Zechariah, who we will read more about in the coming days. These prophets encouraged the people to trust the sovereign and faithful hand of the Lord. They declared that God would be faithful and good. And once again, God moved in the heart of the Persian kings, who provided protection and provision as the work resumed with a renewed zeal.

Chapter 6 ends with the temple being completed and dedicated to the Lord. The Passover was once again celebrated at the temple with sacrifices and worship. God's people even celebrated with believing Gentiles who followed Yahweh and joined the people of God. This joint worship was a symbol and precursor that pointed to Jesus and the unity He would bring later in redemptive history through His ultimate sacrifice. Jesus would defeat sin and death for all people and make a way for every tribe, tongue, and nation to worship the God of creation. Though the journey for the remnant was not easy, we can imagine that the great joy they felt as they worshiped in the rebuilt temple eclipsed all the discouragement and doubt they faced along the way. The same can be said for believers today. Even when our faith seems difficult and opposition crowds in, we can remember our service to the King of kings will always be worth it. Following the Lord does not guarantee an easy journey, but we can be confident that His faithfulness is sure.

> *This was the Lord's work, and He would remain faithful to His remnant.*

THE REBUILDING OF THE TEMPLE WAS DELAYED FOR ABOUT FIFTEEN YEARS. HOW DO YOU THINK THE EXILES FELT DURING THIS TIME? HOW DO YOU RESPOND IN SEASONS OF WAITING? HOW CAN THIS ACCOUNT OF THE EXILES' RETURN HELP YOU REMEMBER GOD'S SOVEREIGNTY?

HAVE YOU EVER EXPERIENCED OPPOSITION BECAUSE OF YOUR FAITH? WHAT WAS YOUR RESPONSE? HOW DID GOD USE THAT SITUATION FOR YOUR GOOD AND HIS GLORY?

HOW WAS GOD'S FAITHFULNESS ON FULL DISPLAY AS THE PEOPLE CELEBRATED PASSOVER FOR THE FIRST TIME AT THE NEWLY BUILT TEMPLE?

Haggai 1-2

TODAY, WE TAKE A BREAK FROM EZRA TO READ THE WORDS OF ONE OF THE PROPHETS WHO SPOKE GOD'S WORD TO THE PEOPLE DURING THIS POINT IN REDEMPTIVE HISTORY.

As we read yesterday in Ezra 5:1 and 6:14, the prophet Haggai was among the exiles who returned to Jerusalem. As they were rebuilding the temple, the Lord gave a message to Haggai to share with His people. This message was to put the Lord first. Haggai takes us back to the time period when opposition arose, and the building of the temple stopped for almost fifteen years. During this time, people chose to focus on rebuilding their own homes and neglected the Lord's house. Haggai confronted this tension.

Haggai shared with the people that the Lord wanted them to consider their ways and search their hearts. God desires to be present with His people, and the temple was the physical manifestation of His dwelling with them. Haggai reminded the people that if the Lord does not dwell with His people, there is no point in building anything else (Haggai 1:7-9).

Haggai called the people to be obedient to God. No matter what they faced from their foes, the Lord would be with them, and it was time for them to stop building for themselves and build a house for the Lord. Haggai's call for the people's obedience is evident in Haggai 1:7, which says, "The Lord of Armies says this: 'Think carefully about your ways.'" Haggai's urging for Judah to remember the Lord's dwelling place should cause us to rejoice that the Lord is so intimately present with us, and it should remind us to place Him on the throne of our hearts.

God chose Zerubbabel to lead the people in obeying the Lord and rebuilding the temple. Though he was not a king and served only as the governor, Zerubbabel was from the line of David and served the Lord faithfully. He did what God had called him to do, and God saw his faithfulness. Zerubbabel would not be forgotten, and his name would be recorded in the genealogy of Jesus (Matthew 1:12–13, Luke 3:27). His life was an intricate piece of the story of redemption, all because he was faithful. Zerubbabel's obedience to God was a glimmer of hope for the line of David. God had not forgotten His promise to David (2 Samuel 7:12–13), and his royal line would remain intact as the people grew ever closer to the promised Messiah's glorious arrival. While Zerubbabel's faithfulness allowed the people to worship and dwell with God through a temple, Jesus's faithfulness gives all of His people complete access to the Lord forever.

God desires to be present with His people.

HAGGAI'S MESSAGE WAS ONE OF ADMONISHMENT BUT ALSO ENCOURAGEMENT FOR THE PEOPLE TO THINK ABOUT THEIR WAYS AND INTENTIONS. WHAT HAVE YOU BEEN NEGLECTING IN YOUR WALK WITH THE LORD?

Some examples could be Bible reading, prayer, or gathering with a church community. How can you get back on the right track and build your life around the Lord?

THE LORD DESIRED A PLACE TO DWELL AMONG HIS PEOPLE. READ EPHESIANS 2:19–22. HOW ARE BELIEVERS NOW A PART OF THIS DWELLING?

THE LINE OF DAVID HAD REMAINED INTACT THROUGH THE EXILE AND THE RETURN TO JERUSALEM. HOW DOES THIS ENCOURAGE YOU TO REMEMBER GOD NEVER ABANDONS HIS CHILDREN AND HAS A PLAN FOR EACH ONE?

Zechariah 1-6

ZECHARIAH WAS A PROPHET WHO SERVED ALONGSIDE THE PROPHET HAGGAI DURING THE RETURN OF THE EXILES (EZRA 5:1, 6:14).

Zechariah encouraged the people to continue rebuilding the temple but declared that first, they must return to the Lord. The people needed to repent and then turn from their sin. If they returned, God would return to them. The people chose to repent and listen, so the Lord gave Zechariah eight visions meant to encourage them and help them persevere in their return from exile.

In Zechariah's first two visions, the Lord tells His people that His favor has come back upon Jerusalem. He will establish it and let it be rebuilt. The vision of the four horns revealed that the nations who scattered the Lord's people would face judgment. Zechariah's vision of a man with a measuring line taking the city's width and length reveals that Jerusalem will be inhabited without walls because the Lord Himself will defend her and be her glory. And while nations would be punished for their mistreatment of God's people, the city of Jerusalem would someday draw the nations of the world to its doors because of the presence of the Lord.

In chapter 3, we see an incredible vision of the Lord that points to the coming of Jesus, the Great High Priest. Zechariah sees the high priest named Joshua wearing filthy garments and being accused by Satan. The Lord rebukes Satan and gives clean garments to Joshua. God tells Joshua that this is a sign of the Branch to come. On the appointed day, Jesus, the final High Priest, will take away the sins of His people by offering His life as a sacrifice on the cross.

The vision of the flying scroll and the woman in a basket in chapter 5 reveals how the Lord removes and deals with sin. Iniquity would have no place in God's restored city. This vision ultimately speaks of the heavenly city of Jerusalem, where sin and evil will forever be destroyed. The vision of the four chariots in chapter 6 also shows us that evil will not be allowed to dwell freely. The Lord will send out His forces to deal with nations who are idolatrous and wicked. God's people will dwell safely and securely in His land, and they will have no reason to fear.

As the passage ends, we see that a crown is placed on Joshua's head and then taken off and taken to the temple. This was a symbolic reminder that no earthly king or priest deserved a crown, but one day, Jesus the Messiah, the King of kings, the Righteous Branch, will reign forever.

> Jesus the Messiah, the King of kings, the Righteous Branch, will reign forever.

WHY WAS IT IMPORTANT FOR THE PEOPLE TO REPENT AND NOT LIVE AS THEIR ANCESTORS HAD? WHY IS IT IMPORTANT FOR YOU TO REPENT OF SIN ON A REGULAR BASIS AS WELL?

READ HEBREWS 10:19–23. HOW DOES CHRIST FULFILL THE ROLE OF THE HIGH PRIEST AND PROVIDE US WITH DIRECT ACCESS TO THE FATHER?

IN WHAT WAYS DO ZECHARIAH'S VISIONS PROVIDE ENCOURAGEMENT, EVEN TODAY, AS BELIEVERS AWAIT CHRIST'S RETURN AND THE END OF ALL EVIL?

Zechariah 7-10

AFTER ZECHARIAH'S VISIONS, THE PEOPLE QUESTIONED WHICH FASTS THEY SHOULD CONTINUE SINCE SOME OF THE THINGS FOR WHICH THEY FASTED ALREADY CAME TO FRUITION.

However, God did not just want His people to focus on rules and religious traditions; His desire was for their hearts to be solely devoted to Him. The Lord gave the people an example of the kind of obedience He desired. He wanted them to love justice, mercy, and compassion; He did not want them to oppress others (Zechariah 7:8-10). He described how their ancestors had not listened to His call for repentance, so they had been scattered. But in chapter 8, the Lord reminded His people of the return to Jerusalem. He ordained that their fasting be turned into times of feasting and celebration. One day, this peace will be fully restored when Jesus returns to earth and gathers His people together. Our fasting and mourning in this broken creation will be replaced with feasting as we embark on the beginning of a new journey in Christ's eternal kingdom.

Chapters 9-10 are filled with promises of Jesus, the coming Messiah. First, His triumphal entry is predicted in Zechariah 9:9. "Zion" refers to the heavenly city of God, and Zechariah prophesies that the King of Zion would one day enter Jerusalem with righteousness and salvation while seated on a donkey. He would be the one true King, unlike any other king in the world. This entry would show His humility as He entered Jerusalem, the city of God, as a willing servant and sacrifice for His people. We will later read how Zechariah describes Christ's second coming when He appears on a fierce warhorse to vindicate His people (Zechariah 14, Revelation 19:11-16). When Jesus comes again, He will save His people from evil, and His entry will be glorious (Zechariah 9:14-16).

He is then described in Zechariah 10:4 as our cornerstone, which is the first stone laid when building a foundation. He is also described as our tent peg, which shows us that He is safe and secure, and we can place the weight of our burdens on Him. Finally, Zechariah writes that He is our battle bow, which shows that He is our victorious warrior. No matter what we are facing, we can trust and hope in this eternal truth. The promise is sure: Jesus will come and bring His people home (Zechariah 10:10).

> The promise is sure: Jesus will come and bring His people home.

WHAT RELIGIOUS TRADITIONS OR RULES DO YOU FOLLOW TOO CLOSELY AT TIMES? HAVE YOU MADE YOUR FAITH MORE ABOUT THESE TRADITIONS OR RULES THAN ABOUT THE LORD? HOW CAN YOU REFOCUS YOUR HEART ON HIM?

HOW DOES JESUS'S HUMBLE ENTRY ON A DONKEY, PROPHESIED HUNDREDS OF YEARS BEFORE HE CAME, DISPLAY GOD'S COMMITMENT TO REDEMPTION AND HIS SOVEREIGNTY OVER EVERY DETAIL ON EARTH?

MULTIPLE TIMES IN ZECHARIAH AND THROUGHOUT THE OLD TESTAMENT, GOD IS REFERRED TO AS THE LORD OF ARMIES. WHAT HAS THIS MEANT FOR THE PEOPLE OF ISRAEL? WHAT DOES IT MEAN FOR YOU TODAY AS YOU FIGHT THE BATTLE AGAINST SIN?

Zechariah 11–14

"REPENT AND RETURN" CONTINUES TO BE ZECHARIAH'S MESSAGE, JUST AS IT WAS THE MESSAGE OF THE PROPHETS WHO CAME BEFORE HIM.

In chapter 11, Zechariah acts out a prophecy of judgment from the Lord to the people. Zechariah acted as the Lord and shepherded a flock intended for slaughter. This flock represented Israel. Because of the sins of the people and their "shepherds," God would take favor and union from them. The three rejected shepherds are thought to be the prophets, priests, and kings of Israel, while the union taken away represents the enmity between Judah and Israel. Zechariah represents Christ in this scenario as the people would reject them, just as they rejected Jesus. When Zechariah asks for his wages for shepherding the flock, he receives thirty pieces of silver—the same amount that the religious leaders gave Judas for his betrayal of Jesus (Matthew 27:9–10). Thirty pieces of silver was not a small amount of money, but it was not a great amount either. And yet, this represents the small value that God's people put on the prophets' words.

However, in chapter 12, the tone shifts, and we see the glorious future of Israel, God's chosen people. Our God will pour out His Spirit, a Spirit of grace and mercy, and the people who once rejected Him will repent and return at last. God, in His mercy and faithfulness, would redeem His people. In these verses, God describes Himself as the One "whom they pierced" (Zechariah 12:10). This foreshadows the crucifixion, where Jesus took on our sin and died so that all who trust in Him can be saved. Zechariah goes on to describe this Messiah as the shepherd provided by God but struck down, again referring to the death of Christ (Zechariah 13:7). This is the gospel, and we have received God's Spirit of mercy and grace through Jesus.

Chapter 14 announces the day of the Lord when the humble Messiah will become the conquering King. Rivers will flow from Jerusalem, and our God will be King over all. Those who gave their hearts to Christ will worship at the temple in Jerusalem and celebrate the Feast of Tabernacles. Israel and those Gentiles now grafted into the promises will wander no more as they find their home in the glorious new heaven and new earth. God was faithful to redeem His people from exile, and He will be faithful to redeem His people and carry them home, where permanent rest will be forever found in His presence.

> God, in His mercy and faithfulness, would redeem His people.

READ MATTHEW 26:14–16 AND 27:3–10. HOW DO THESE VERSES FULFILL ZECHARIAH 11:12–13?

READ REVELATION 22:1–5. HOW WILL THESE VERSES FULFILL ZECHARIAH 14:6–11?

IN WHAT WAYS WOULD ZECHARIAH'S MESSAGE TO THE EXILES PROVIDE ENCOURAGEMENT? WHAT ENCOURAGEMENT HAS THIS BOOK GIVEN YOU AS YOU CONTINUE TO FOLLOW JESUS?

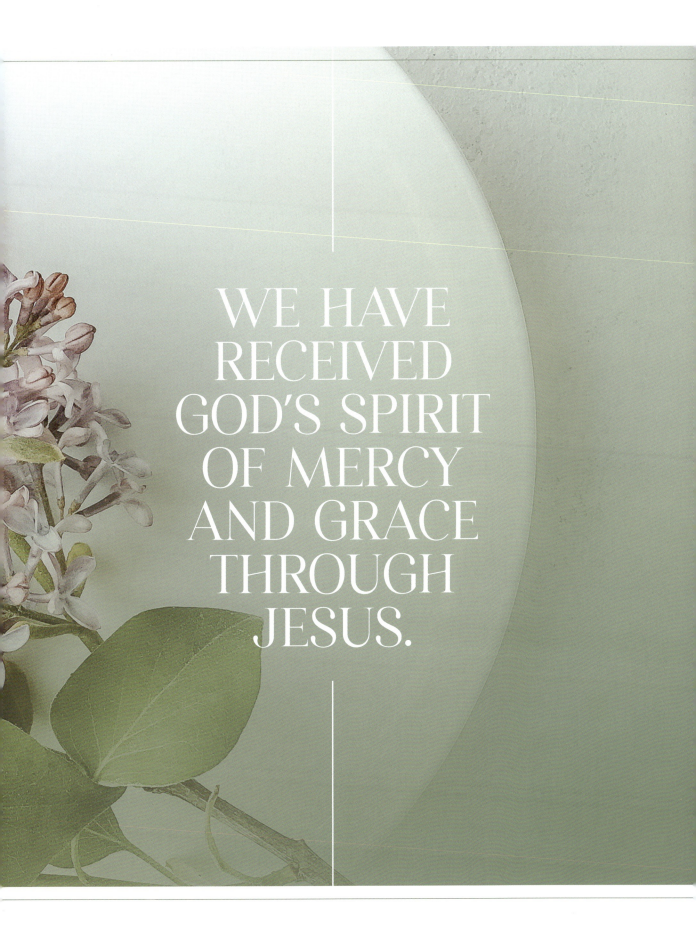

Esther 1–5

THE EVENTS OF ESTHER FALL DURING THE FIFTEEN-YEAR TIME PERIOD WHEN THE REBUILDING OF THE TEMPLE HAD STOPPED.

As Haggai and Zechariah encouraged and prophesied to the people in Jerusalem, many miles away, God was using one woman and her cousin to save the Jewish nation. Esther's story occurs in the capital city of Susa in the Persian empire. Persia had conquered Babylon, thus acquiring the exiled Israelites. The book opens during one of many feasts that take place in the book. During this feast, King Ahasuerus (Xerxes I) commands Queen Vashti to parade in front of a group of intoxicated men as an object for their pleasure. Her refusal to appear sets God's sovereign plan into motion.

The rash king removed Vashti as queen, and the search for a new queen began. From all over the land, virgins were sent—likely involuntary—to the palace. Once there, they were brought before the king, one by one, to satisfy his desires and see if one of them may be the next queen. The weighty realities of this story go beyond the romanticized versions that history has offered. Esther was one in a long list of women who would be concubines in the harem.

Esther found favor with the king and indeed became the queen of Persia. She was an unlikely candidate with a heritage she kept hidden. Esther had been raised by her cousin, Mordecai, and it was their close relationship that enabled Mordecai to warn Esther of an assassination plot against the king. Their close relationship would remain important as the text introduces a man named Haman. Haman hated Mordecai and all Jews, so he created a plot to kill the Jewish people, and the king signed it into law, not realizing he signed his own queen's death warrant.

When Mordecai heard of the plot to kill the Jews, he knew Esther must act. Mordecai trusted that the Lord would find a way to save the Jews and keep His covenant. The Lord placed Esther where she was so He could use her for His glory. Mordecai pleaded with her that perhaps she had become queen "for such a time as this" (Esther 4:14) Esther responded with urgency and immediately asked the people of God to fast on her behalf.

Going before the king uninvited was dangerous, and Esther's life was at stake when she chose to enter the room. But Esther found favor with the king, and he agreed to attend a banquet at her request. Meanwhile, Haman was making plans to kill Mordecai by constructing a gallows to carry out his evil plans. All might seem hopeless at this point in the narrative, but God was working to fulfill His purpose in Esther, Mordecai, and the Jewish people.

God was working to fulfill His purpose in Esther, Mordecai, and the Jewish people.

GOD'S NAME IS NEVER MENTIONED IN THE BOOK OF ESTHER, BUT HIS SOVEREIGNTY IS ON FULL DISPLAY. ONE EXAMPLE OF THIS IS FOUND IN THE FACT THAT KING AHASUERUS WAS NOT A GODLY MAN, BUT GOD STILL USED HIM FOR HIS PURPOSES. HOW DOES THIS SET THE TONE FOR THE BOOK OF ESTHER?

WHAT DOES IT SAY ABOUT MORDECAI'S CHARACTER AND HIS HEART FOR THE LORD THAT HE WOULD SAVE THE LIFE OF THE KING WHO HAD TAKEN HIS COUSIN? HOW DOES THIS TEACH YOU TO LIVE OUT JESUS'S COMMAND IN LUKE 6:27–28?

IN ESTHER 4:14, MORDECAI SAYS TO ESTHER, "WHO KNOWS, PERHAPS YOU HAVE COME TO YOUR ROYAL POSITION FOR SUCH A TIME AS THIS." THINK OF AN UNLIKELY TIME OR PLACE GOD HAS USED YOU. *What can you learn from Esther's story and your own story about God's work behind the scenes? How does it help you trust Him more?*

Esther 1–5

Esther 6–10

GOD CONTINUED HIS PROVIDENTIAL WORK AMONG THOSE IN THE PALACE IN SUSA.

After he received Esther's invitation, the king had trouble sleeping, so he had the book that recorded the kingdom's daily events read to him. As it was read, the king remembered how Mordecai had saved his life. The next day, the king asked Haman for his opinion on the very best way to honor a man. The wicked Haman assumed that the king was going to honor him. Imagine his shock when he finished naming his elaborate plans only to be told to carry them out for Mordecai—the man he wanted dead. Haman returned home mournfully, and then a royal official arrived and rushed him to Queen Esther's banquet.

At the banquet, Esther, in courage and bravery, revealed to the king her heritage and Haman's plot to murder her people, the Jews. Haman begged for his life, but the furious king ordered Haman to be executed on the same gallows he had built for Mordecai. Haman's evil plan was thwarted, and he paid the price that he had intended for Mordecai. The king decreed that when enemies came to attack, the Jews could defend themselves by any means necessary, thus avoiding annihilation. In integrity, and perhaps in memory of their past, the Jews defeated their enemies but did not take the spoils of war. God had not abandoned His people. He brought deliverance and used His people to accomplish it.

The Feast of Purim was inaugurated to celebrate the great victory and joy of that day, and Mordecai was made second to the king. God did what He said He would do—even using a foreign king who did not know God to rescue His people. The hero of this story is not Mordecai or Esther but our great God whom they served. God's name may not be present in this book, but His providence is on display over and over again. God continuously works in ways we cannot see or imagine, yet He still invites us into His story of redemption. Jesus saves us from the annihilation caused by sin. As His redeemed children, we are called to seek and build the kingdom of God on earth. We are called to herald the good news of the gospel to those around us. We are called to be faithful in ordinary places and ordinary days.

> God had not abandoned His people. He brought deliverance and used His people to accomplish it.

GOD PROVIDED VINDICATION FOR MORDECAI, ESTHER, AND THE JEWS WITH THE DEATH OF HAMAN. HOW DOES THIS ENCOURAGE YOU NOT TO SEEK REVENGE BUT TO ALLOW THE LORD TO VINDICATE YOU?

THOUGH THE KING'S ORIGINAL DECREE OF ANNIHILATION COULD NOT BE REVERSED, GOD PROVIDED A WAY FOR THE JEWISH PEOPLE TO DEFEND THEMSELVES WITH THE SECOND DECREE.
How has God provided a way out of a difficult situation in your own life?
How has He proven trustworthy, even when it seemed like there was no way out?

ESTHER WAS FAITHFUL RIGHT WHERE GOD HAD PLACED HER.
HOW CAN YOU SHOW FAITHFULNESS TO GOD'S CALL IN YOUR EVERYDAY LIFE?

Ezra 7-10

WE BRIEFLY LEFT THE BOOK OF EZRA TO EXAMINE THE ACCOUNTS OF HAGGAI, ZECHARIAH, AND ESTHER, AS THE EVENTS IN EACH OF THESE BOOKS OCCURRED DURING THE FIFTEEN-YEAR PAUSE OF THE TEMPLE REBUILD.

We rejoin Ezra's narrative in chapter 7 after the temple's completion and as a new wave of exiles returned to Jerusalem. The text begins with Ezra's family history and his occupation as a scribe. Multiple times throughout the remainder of the book, a key phrase describes Ezra. The text states that "the hand of the Lord his God was upon him" (Ezra 7:6). Though we do not have many details about Ezra's background, these words help us understand the kind of man he was. The king of Persia at that time, Artaxerxes, sent Ezra and all who wished to accompany him to Jerusalem. The king gave them protection and financial aid in accomplishing this great task. As the people began to journey, Ezra, along with the Levites he identified, fasted and prayed for protection on the journey. The Lord's hand was indeed upon Ezra as he led the people to Jerusalem.

Upon their arrival to Jerusalem, Ezra and the newly arrived exiles offered burnt offerings and worshiped the Lord. God had provided safety and brought the people home, just as He promised long ago. Sadly, the Israelites who had inhabited the land before them had begun following their own desires. God had commanded His people not to marry foreigners in order to prevent their hearts from turning to other gods. With the realization of the sin of Israel, Ezra prayed. He confessed and wept as he asked God for mercy. The confession shown in this passage is both corporate and personal. The people confessed their personal sins, but they also confessed the sins of their nation and even those of their ancestors who had lived wickedly. Despite all of their sin and brokenness, the Lord their God had not forsaken His people. He had extended His steadfast, covenant love to them and had been with them every step of the way.

The end of the book finds the people repenting and making some hard decisions about how to move forward in the issue of intermarriage. Many Bible scholars disagree about whether the decisions that were made were based on God's direction or the people's zeal. However, what is clear is that God's people were once again learning a hard lesson and recognizing that God's ways are for their own good. The book of Ezra points us to Jesus and urges us to be faithful to the One who is always faithful to us.

> The Lord's hand was indeed upon Ezra as he led the people to Jerusalem.

EZRA 7:10 SAYS, "NOW EZRA HAD DETERMINED IN HIS HEART TO STUDY THE LAW OF THE LORD, OBEY IT, AND TEACH ITS STATUTES AND ORDINANCES IN ISRAEL." WHAT CAN YOU LEARN FROM EZRA'S DETERMINATION TO STUDY, OBEY, AND TEACH THE WORD?

Read Psalm 119:47–48, and make this your prayer throughout your day.

BEFORE EZRA LED THE PEOPLE BACK TO JERUSALEM, THEY FASTED AND PRAYED FOR THEIR JOURNEY. HAVE YOU EVER FASTED? HOW DOES FASTING POINT YOUR HEART TO CHRIST?

DO YOU MOURN YOUR SIN AND THE SIN OF YOUR FAMILY AS EZRA AND THE PEOPLE OF ISRAEL DID? HOW MIGHT TRUE REPENTANCE CHANGE THE SINFUL PATTERNS IN YOUR LIFE?

Nehemiah 1–3

THE BOOK OF NEHEMIAH FALLS NEAR THE MIDDLE OF OUR BIBLES, YET, CHRONOLOGICALLY, IT IS ONE OF THE FINAL PIECES OF THE OLD TESTAMENT STORY.

Its main character is a man named Nehemiah, yet many scholars believe that this book was written by Ezra. That said, the events in Nehemiah take place about fifteen years after the events recorded in the book of Ezra. While the book of Ezra details the rebuilding of the temple, the book of Nehemiah details the rebuilding of the wall of Jerusalem.

The account begins in Susa with a report coming back to Nehemiah about the state of Jerusalem. Nehemiah was a Jew working in the Persian palace as the cupbearer to the king. This position has been likened to the modern "chief of staff." When Nehemiah heard about the "great trouble and disgrace" of Jerusalem (Nehemiah 1:3), he was moved with compassion and turned to prayer. He wept and prayed because of the great need that he saw. Nehemiah was clearly distraught by this news—not just for a moment but for an extended period of time. In fact, it was at least four months until King Artaxerxes noticed Nehemiah's sadness of heart and Nehemiah got the opportunity to present his request before the king.

In faith, Nehemiah went to the Lord in prayer, and in faith, he went to the king with a bold request. Nehemiah requested assistance to go to Jerusalem to rebuild the wall. The king granted his request, and once again, in faith, Nehemiah followed the Lord as he journeyed back to Jerusalem and rallied the people to join him in rebuilding the city wall for God's glory.

Though the Lord tasked Nehemiah with this great work, Nehemiah was not immune to opposition. Opposition would come, and the task before him would at times feel too great. Nehemiah would need to rebuild the wall meant to protect Jerusalem, and he would need to encourage a very discouraged group of people to join him in the work. Yet, by chapter 3, in what may seem like a long list of names, we see that the people of God worked together to accomplish the mission of God. Nehemiah is a small book of the Bible, yet in it, we are reminded to look at the needs around us and respond in compassion. We are reminded to come to the Lord in prayer and to humbly lead others to love and serve the Lord as well. Most of all, we are pointed to Jesus, who has compassion on us, prays for us, leads us, and is the true restorer of His people.

> In faith, Nehemiah followed the Lord as he journeyed back to Jerusalem.

DO YOU PRAY FOR YOUR CHRISTIAN BROTHERS AND SISTERS AROUND THE WORLD? HOW CAN YOU CULTIVATE A LIFE OF PRAYER TO INTERCEDE ON BEHALF OF THOSE WHO EXPERIENCE HARDSHIP FOR THEIR FAITH, JUST AS NEHEMIAH DID FOR JERUSALEM?

IN NEHEMIAH 2:6, WE SEE THE KING AND QUEEN ASK NEHEMIAH WHEN HE WILL RETURN. HE WAS OBVIOUSLY A TRUSTED AND LOVED SERVANT. HOW DOES NEHEMIAH'S CHARACTER BEFORE A LOST KING AND QUEEN ENCOURAGE YOU TO LIVE A GODLY LIFE BEFORE UNBELIEVERS?

CHAPTER 3 REMINDS US THAT ALL JOBS FOR THE KINGDOM ARE IMPORTANT. HOW ARE YOU SERVING IN YOUR CHURCH CURRENTLY? HOW CAN YOU USE YOUR GIFTS TO GLORIFY GOD AND SERVE OTHERS?

Nehemiah 4-6

NEHEMIAH AND THE PEOPLE GOT TO WORK REBUILDING THE WALL.

But it would not be a completely smooth process. It did not take long for opposition to arrive through Sanballat and Tobiah. They came with insults and accusations. Nehemiah's response should not be a surprise after what we have read about him so far. His response was to go to the Lord in prayer. He prayed, and the building continued. Nehemiah and his fellow laborers did not let the schemes of their enemies distract them from the work that God called them to do.

Those rebuilding the wall had a very real fear, but they went to the Lord and prayed for Him to be with them. They remembered the Lord, and by faith in the God who had never left them, they overcame the obstacles set before them. But the opposition did not only come from the outside. There was also the opposition of sin within the people. It came to light that many were oppressing the poor. Nehemiah became angry upon learning this news. Yet, instead of reacting in anger, he reacted with confession. Personal and corporate confession came from the lips of Nehemiah in prayer once again. The end of chapter 5 describes the wealth and generosity of Nehemiah and explains how he used his wealth to bless those around him and continue God's work.

Chapter 6 chronicles the further intimidation of Nehemiah from Sanballat, Tobiah, and Geshem as Nehemiah neared the competition of the wall. The Lord gave Nehemiah great discernment to avoid the tactics used by these men to harm his reputation before the people. Despite their schemes and plots, Nehemiah and the exiles completed the wall in just fifty-two days. With the building of the wall complete, the book shifts to the building of God's people.

When we are serving the Lord, opposition will come. The attacks of the enemy can leave us feeling crippled with fear and discourage us from doing what God has called us to do. In his wisdom, Nehemiah encouraged the people to press on and continue the work they had been sent to do. Nehemiah turned to the Lord in prayer and was confident that the Lord would fight for them. God's people did not have to fear or be discouraged because the Lord was on their side. Those who follow Christ have no need to fear either. Jesus conquered fear on the cross, and we have Him as our shield and comfort through any opposition that comes our way.

> God's people did not have to fear or be discouraged because the Lord was on their side.

HAVE YOU EVER EXPERIENCED OPPOSITION BECAUSE OF YOUR FAITH? HOW DID YOU RESPOND? HOW DOES GOD WANT YOU TO RESPOND IN THE FACE OF OPPOSITION?

BUILDING THE WALL SEEMED LIKE AN INSURMOUNTABLE TASK, BUT GOD WAS WITH THEM TO BRING IT TO COMPLETION. WHAT SEEMS INSURMOUNTABLE IN YOUR LIFE RIGHT NOW? USE THE SPACE BELOW TO CONFESS YOUR FEARS, AND ASK GOD FOR STRENGTH AND WISDOM TO ENABLE YOU TO PRESS ON.

NEHEMIAH 6:16 SAYS, "WHEN ALL OUR ENEMIES HEARD THIS, ALL THE SURROUNDING NATIONS WERE INTIMIDATED AND LOST THEIR CONFIDENCE, FOR THEY REALIZED THAT THIS TASK HAD BEEN ACCOMPLISHED BY OUR GOD."

How does this give you courage as you set out to do what God has called you to do?

Nehemiah 7–10

GOD HAD GIVEN NEHEMIAH AND THE PEOPLE THE STRENGTH TO FINISH BUILDING THE WALL, BUT HE WAS NOT FINISHED BUILDING HIS PEOPLE.

God called Nehemiah to assemble the people, and chapter 7 provides a numbering of the returned exiles. As the book shifts from the building of the wall to the building of the people, the text points out the necessity of the Word of God. A renewed passion for God's Word is a prerequisite to revival.

In chapter 8, the people listened to Scripture read aloud from morning until midday, and they wept in response to the Word as they realized their sin and understood their deep need for redemption. Prayer and the reading and teaching of God's Word were foundational to the transformation of the people of God. Nehemiah points out that the joy of the Lord is their strength (Nehemiah 8:10). The people spent much time and energy building a wall around Jerusalem, but the Lord wanted them to know that He alone was their strength, refuge, fortress, and stronghold.

As the people opened the Word of God, they saw the commandment for the Feast of Booths, and they celebrated this feast together. Chapter 9 is a beautiful account of a day-long worship service. This time of worship began with the confession of their personal sin and their sin as a nation. Together, they read the Word of God for hours and clung to every word of Scripture. And then they prayed. The majority of chapter 9 is a prayer—one that tells the story of the faithfulness of God and the wandering of His people. Though they rebelled against Him, God came near to His people over and over again. The covenant promises of Nehemiah 9 are fulfilled in Jesus. He is the Redeemer who was promised to Abraham long ago, the One whom the prophets of old proclaimed, and the One to whom every verse of Scripture points. He is forever faithful to fulfill His promises.

After the worship and revival of chapter 9, chapter 10 records the signing of the covenant. The people who had wept over their sin and worshiped the Lord for His faithfulness now surrendered to Him. They surrendered their lives, and they surrendered to His commands. This was a call to action as the people stepped up to declare their loyalty to Yahweh. Jesus asks the same for all those who come to Him. Salvation leads to surrender. The gospel leads to action. We serve the Lord with joy, for He is faithful to all generations.

> Though they rebelled against Him, God came near to His people over and over again.

DO YOU TRULY LOVE GOD'S WORD? DO YOU WEEP IN RESPONSE TO YOUR SIN AND YOUR NEED FOR REDEMPTION? IN WHAT WAYS CAN YOU CULTIVATE A DEEPER LOVE FOR SCRIPTURE AND ALLOW IT TO CHANGE YOUR HEART?

THE ISRAELITES' DAY-LONG WORSHIP SERVICE REMINDS US THAT OUR LIVES ARE MEANT TO BE A SACRIFICE OF PRAISE TO THE LORD. WHAT STEPS CAN YOU TAKE IN YOUR EVERYDAY LIFE TO WORSHIP THE LORD IN ALL YOU DO? (HINT: READ COLOSSIANS 3:17.)

BELIEVERS MAKE A BINDING CONTRACT WITH THE LORD WHEN THEY FOLLOW CHRIST. READ EPHESIANS 1:13–14. HOW IS OUR CONTRACT SEALED? IN LIGHT OF THIS, HOW SHOULD YOU LIVE?

Nehemiah 11–13
Psalm 126

AS WE TURN TO NEHEMIAH 11–12, WE SEE THE CITY OF JERUSALEM RESETTLED.

Many people chose to leave their land and their homes to come and help populate Jerusalem and build the kingdom of God. While the lists of names are seemingly long and tedious to read, for the people in Nehemiah's day, this was important as they were counted in their faithfulness to the Lord. The names of the faithful were written down, and God's people rejoiced to see their names listed as those who were obedient to the Lord. The wall was dedicated, and it was a time of joy and rejoicing for all that the Lord had done.

Psalm 126 is a song of rejoicing, likely written after the return of the exiles. God had graciously restored Jerusalem with the rebuilding of the temple and the completion of the wall. The people had returned to inhabit the city of David and worship the Lord once again. Psalm 126:5 says, "Those who sow in tears will reap with shouts of joy." The exiles had indeed sowed many tears, but the Lord was ever faithful and fulfilled His promise to restore them to the land. This psalm is the seventh of fifteen pilgrimage songs—called the Songs of Ascent—that the Israelites sang for hundreds of years at the annual festivals in Jerusalem. Psalm 126 is a psalm of joy, remembrance, and restoration—one that will find it is ultimate completion in Christ in the new heaven and new earth.

Though Nehemiah 12 ends triumphantly in Jerusalem with the people greatly rejoicing, chapter 13 flashes forward over a decade, and the result is discouraging. Nehemiah had returned to his service in the palace of Artaxerxes. Sadly, he receives a report that the people had once again wandered from the Lord and were unfaithful to the covenant. Nehemiah received a leave of absence to return to Jerusalem, purify the temple, and bring reform to the people. The Lord had been steadfast and faithful to them, yet still, they wandered. While this might not be surprising given their history, it is a sobering reminder that we are all prone to sin and must keep our hearts fixed on the Lord.

The people's broken covenant reminds us that only God keeps His covenants perfectly. We will try and fail at every turn. Jesus is the lasting covenant all people awaited. He alone provides us with hearts that desire to love and serve the Lord. The book of Nehemiah calls us to faithfulness and surrender. It points to the great things that can be accomplished for the Lord, but ultimately, it reminds us that it is only through the power of Jesus that our faithfulness to Him is possible.

> Only God keeps His covenants perfectly.

THINK OF A DIFFICULT SEASON THAT GOD DELIVERED YOU FROM. HOW DID YOU PRAISE HIM AND CELEBRATE HIS GOODNESS IN YOUR LIFE? HOW CAN YOU MAKE THAT A PATTERN, NO MATTER WHAT YOU GO THROUGH?

IN WHAT WAYS ARE YOU PRONE TO WANDER FROM THE LORD? WHAT STEPS OF ACCOUNTABILITY CAN BE PUT IN PLACE TO KEEP YOUR HEART FOCUSED ON GOD?

CHRONOLOGICALLY, NEHEMIAH IS ONE OF THE FINAL ACCOUNTS IN THE OLD TESTAMENT. TAKE SOME TIME TO THINK ABOUT HOW YOU HAVE WITNESSED GOD'S FAITHFULNESS FROM GENESIS TO THE RETURN OF THE EXILES. HOW DOES THIS ENCOURAGE YOU AND REMIND YOU TO TRUST IN OUR SOVEREIGN GOD?

Malachi 1–4

AS WE REACH THE END OF THE OLD TESTAMENT, WE READ ONE OF THE ONLY MESSAGES GIVEN TO THE EXILES AFTER THEIR RETURN FROM CAPTIVITY.

Though the people did not know it, this was God's final message to them for many years. The people had been given numerous chances to turn to the Lord, but they remained stubborn in their sin. Malachi begins by sharing God's great love for His people, and their immediate response was to question how God had loved them. What a sad response from the people God had chosen to bestow His favor and grace upon. He loved them faithfully, yet they scoffed at His love.

Malachi addresses how this lack of love for the Lord had deeply affected the people. The priests, the spiritual leaders of Israel, dishonored the Lord by accepting polluted sacrifices. The Lord rebuked the priests for leading the people astray and corrupting the original covenant of Levi. Israel was also breaking the covenant of marriage, which was sacred to the Lord. By doing so, they brought destruction upon their families, and they revealed their lack of respect for the Lord. The sins Malachi describes are heavy, but they are also all too common today. We are quick to doubt His love, give our second best, and not honor our commitments—yet our God loves us still and calls us to repent and return.

Chapter 3 begins with a prophecy of two messengers. The first prophesied messenger is John the Baptist. Jesus affirmed that John was the messenger of the covenant in Matthew 11:7–15. The second messenger is the Lord Himself. Jesus, God in the flesh, would come to the temple and be the refiner for the people's sins. Jesus came to free us from sin and bring us to the Father. In the last half of the chapter, God makes it clear to the people that they were guilty of robbing Him. They had promised to give to the Lord, and then they did not. God pleaded with them to do right and also reminded them that they were not only robbing God but themselves. They were missing out on God's blessing.

The book closes by reminding the people to remember the law of Moses and then to watch for the prophet Elijah. While Moses represents all of the Law and Elijah represents all of the prophets, Jesus would be the fulfillment of all of the Law and everything the prophets spoke about. But for now, for the next four hundred years, there will be silence—a silence that will continue until Christ bursts onto the scene and changes everything.

> Jesus came to free us from sin and bring us to the Father.

IN WHAT WAYS HAVE YOU QUESTIONED GOD'S LOVE FOR YOU? LIKE ISRAEL, HOW HAS HE PROVEN HIMSELF FAITHFUL OVER AND OVER IN YOUR LIFE? WHY CAN YOU TRUST HIM?

HOW HAVE YOU ROBBED GOD? HOW DOES GIVING TO THE LORD AND HIS CHURCH DEMONSTRATE YOUR RELIANCE ON HIM?

GOD WOULD BE SILENT FOR OVER FOUR HUNDRED YEARS BEFORE SENDING HIS GREATEST GIFT. READ MATTHEW 5:17 AND LUKE 24:44. HOW DOES JESUS FULFILL MALACHI'S MESSAGE AND THE ENTIRE MESSAGE OF THE OLD TESTAMENT?

What is the Gospel?

Thank you for reading and enjoying this study with us! We are abundantly grateful for the Word of God, the instruction we glean from it, and the ever-growing understanding it provides for us of God's character. We are also thankful that Scripture continually points to one thing in innumerable ways: the gospel.

We remember our brokenness when we read about the fall of Adam and Eve in the garden of Eden (Genesis 3), where sin entered into a perfect world and maimed it. We remember the necessity that something innocent must die to pay for our sin when we read about the atoning sacrifices in the Old Testament. We read that we have all sinned and fallen short of the glory of God (Romans 3:23) and that the penalty for our brokenness, the wages of our sin, is death (Romans 6:23). We all need grace and mercy, but most importantly, we all need a Savior.

We consider the goodness of God when we realize that He did not plan to leave us in this dire state. We see His promise to buy us back from the clutches of sin and death in Genesis 3:15. And we see that promise accomplished with Jesus Christ on the cross. Jesus Christ knew no sin yet became sin so that we might become righteous through His sacrifice (2 Corinthians 5:21). Jesus was tempted in every way that we are and lived sinlessly. He was reviled yet still yielded Himself for our sake, that we may have life abundant in Him. Jesus lived the perfect life that we could not live and died the death that we deserved.

The gospel is profound yet simple. There are many mysteries in it that we will never understand this side of heaven, but there is still overwhelming weight to its implications in this life. The gospel tells of our sinfulness and God's goodness and a gracious gift that compels a response. We are saved by grace through faith, which means that we rest with faith in the grace that Jesus Christ displayed on the cross (Ephesians 2:8-9). We cannot save ourselves from our brokenness or do any amount of good works to merit God's favor. Still, we can have faith that what Jesus accomplished in His death, burial, and resurrection was more than enough for our salvation and our eternal delight. When we accept God, we are commanded to die to ourselves and our sinful desires and live a life worthy of the calling we have received (Ephesians 4:1). The gospel compels us to be sanctified, and in so doing, we are conformed to the likeness of Christ Himself. This is hope. This is redemption. This is the gospel.

Scriptures to reference:

GENESIS 3:15	*I will put hostility between you and the woman, and between your offspring and her offspring. He will strike your head, and you will strike his heel.*
ROMANS 3:23	*For all have sinned and fall short of the glory of God.*
ROMANS 6:23	*For the wages of sin is death, but the gift of God is eternal life in Christ Jesus our Lord.*
2 CORINTHIANS 5:21	*He made the one who did not know sin to be sin for us, so that in him we might become the righteousness of God.*
EPHESIANS 2:8-9	*For you are saved by grace through faith, and this is not from yourselves; it is God's gift—not from works, so that no one can boast.*
EPHESIANS 4:1-3	*Therefore I, the prisoner in the Lord, urge you to walk worthy of the calling you have received, with all humility and gentleness, with patience, bearing with one another in love, making every effort to keep the unity of the Spirit through the bond of peace.*

This is hope.
This is redemption.
This is the gospel.

*Thank you for studying
God's Word with us!*

CONNECT WITH US

@thedailygraceco

@dailygracepodcast

CONTACT US

info@thedailygraceco.com

SHARE

#thedailygraceco

VISIT US ONLINE

www.thedailygraceco.com

MORE DAILY GRACE

The Daily Grace App

Daily Grace Podcast